JOE LOUIS
THE BROWN BOMBER

JOE LOUIS

THE BROWN BOMBER

BILL LIBBY

Lothrop, Lee & Shepard Books
New York

Title-page photo: Joe Louis in 1934, shortly after he turned pro. (*UPI*)

All other photos are from the author's collection.

 Inquiries should be addressed to Lothrop, Lee & Shepard Books, a division of William Morrow & Company, Inc., 105 Madison Avenue, New York, New York 10016.
Printed in the United States of America.
First Edition
1 2 3 4 5 6 7 8 9 10

Library of Congress Cataloging in Publication Data

Libby, Bill.
Joe Louis, The Brown Bomber.

Includes index.
SUMMARY: The life story of Joe Louis, heavyweight champion boxer, with the complete history of his career in the ring.
1. Louis, Joe, 1914- —Juvenile literature. 2. Boxers (Sports)—United States—Biography—Juvenile literature. [1. Louis, Joe, 1914- 2. Boxers (Sports) 3. Afro-Americans—Biography] I. Title.
GV1132.L6L5 796.8'3'0924 [B] [92] 80-12372
ISBN 0-688-41968-2 ISBN 0-688-51968-7 (lib. bdg.)

DEDICATION

To the doctors,
who were there when I needed them:
To Bill Klein, his wife Shelley,
and their sons Russell, Ryan, and Keith,
all of whom are my friends.
To Alan Hermer,
who helped when needed.
And to Lloyd Singer, his wife Sue,
and their children Howie, Scott, Lori, and Carol Anne,
the most treasured of friends.

ALSO BY BILL LIBBY

THE REGGIE JACKSON STORY

CONTENTS

1

CLASSIC CONTEST

It was June of 1941 and Joe Louis was at the peak of his incredible career. He had just turned 27 years of age and was in his eighth year as a professional boxer. He had won the heavyweight title four years earlier to the month and was defending it for the eighteenth time. He had defended it successfully with five knockouts in the preceding five months of the year. He was a fighting champion the likes of which have not been seen at any other time.

It may seem like a long time ago, and it was, but it does not seem so to those who watched "The Brown Bomber" in awesome action in person, or on film in the movie theaters after his fights, or who listened with the rest of the world to the exciting radio broadcasts of his bouts in the 1930s and 1940s before he came back from retirement and came crashing to earth as a mere mortal in the 1950s.

It does not seem so long ago to those who consider him the finest fighter of all time. More than forty years after his finest fights he was recognized wherever he went and hailed as a hero. In his declining years of the 1970s he was given standing ovations whenever he made a public appearance. No other athlete, except maybe Babe Ruth—not even Jack Dempsey or Red Grange, Bobby Jones or Bill Tilden, Ty Cobb or Joe DiMaggio, Arnold Palmer or Wilt Chamberlain, O. J. Simpson or Muhammad Ali—ever made such an impact on the sporting public. Even those who did not care about sports listened excitedly to broadcasts of his bouts.

He was, of course, a mortal, as imperfect as any of us. Born in the cotton fields of Alabama and reared in the black ghettos of Detroit, he was a simple, almost uneducated man, but he spoke with surprising wisdom. When he donated all his money from two title fights to Armed Forces charities during World War II and was asked why he fought for nothing, he said, "I'm not fighting for nothing. I'm fighting for my country." It is said that with his skill and simple honesty he did more for blacks than any athlete who ever lived, but when it was said that he was a credit to his race, a sportswriter added, "He is a credit to his race—the human race."

He was a mortal who went through three marriages and almost five million dollars in ring earnings and wound up poor and in terrible tax troubles, but somehow he seemed superhuman. He knocked out foe after foe with perhaps the most powerful punches the ring has seen, and held his title longer and defended it more often than any other boxing king ever crowned.

Boxing is a savage sport and it is not easy to survive

in it. The best do not always win easily and although Joe Louis may have been the best, it was not easy for him that night in June of 1941 when as heavyweight champion he boxed Billy Conn in one of several classic contests "The Brown Bomber" had during his career, one that illustrates his strengths and weaknesses as well as any.

Billy Conn was a cocky kid of 23, out of Pittsburgh. He had given up his light heavyweight title to go after the heavyweight crown and was 25 pounds lighter than Louis. But he was three years younger and a great deal faster afoot than Louis. Conn had fast hands and hit hard. Louis could be knocked down and had been by several foes, though he usually got up to knock them out. He had been beaten by only one opponent, Max Schmeling, and knocked him out in one round in their rematch. Conn was superior as a stylist, but, as Louis said, "He can run, but he can't hide." Louis was not fast afoot, but he had fast hands and hit harder than Conn or anyone else. He kept shuffling forward, jarring foes with a lethal left jab, following with straight rights and left hooks. When he hit them, he hurt them. And once he hurt foes, he finished them off faster than any other ringman ever. He was one of the few who could knock out an opponent with one punch.

A crowd of more than 50,000 fans filled the Polo Grounds baseball park for their fight, paying close to half a million dollars to see the bout. Louis had fights which drew larger crowds and made more money, but he was a 3–1 favorite this night. Few realized that "The Pittsburgh Kid" was as good as he was or as much of a threat to the champ as he was. A heavyweight title fight in a big ballpark outdoors is one of the most thrilling things in sports, and the fans hushed momentarily as all the lights darkened, except those spotlighting the two foes, and all awaited the opening bell. Standing almost six-foot-two, weighing just under 200 pounds, Louis stood expressionless, as always, in his corner. The six-foot, 175-pound Conn danced a little dance, waiting. Unlike a ballgame, a fight can end suddenly, in seconds, on a knockout, or can go to the limit of 15 rounds to a decision, so the tension is terrific. The fans started to holler as the bell rang and the title fight started.

Most of Louis's foes seemed scared simply entering the ring with Joe. Although he was considered a cocky Irishman, Conn seemed jittery and unsure of himself in the first round. As Joe moved in, Billy backed off. Joe would jab and hook and Billy would duck inside and hang on until referee Eddie Joseph broke them apart. Joe threw a long right and Conn, ducking, stumbled and slipped to the canvas as the crowd came to its feet, hollering. He hadn't been hit and it was no knockdown, but Billy looked bad as he got up and resumed running the rest of the round.

In the second round Conn began to box a bit, but still kept jumping away as though jittery. Louis reached him with some long right hands, but late in the round Conn began to counter with return rights of his own. Louis thought he was pressing in for the kill. "I thought I was reaching him. I thought I had him. I thought it would be only another round or two," Louis remembered later. But Billy recalled, "I was beginning to get my confidence back and box like I can. He's such a big man it's no wonder I was nervous to start with, but I began to talk to myself and tell myself I was the best and I could beat this guy if I boxed like I could."

Reaching his rhythm, Billy began to box brilliantly in the third. He'd jab and duck punches, duck punches and hook, moving in and out. Near round's end he pinned Louis to the ropes and flurried with both hands as the crowd came back to its feet, surprised and screaming. In the fourth, Billy lashed out with long rights that landed and a left to the pit of the stomach that seemed to hurt the champion. The crowd was screaming; Joe was missing with his short, strong punches. In his corner, Joe's trainer, Jack Blackburn, warned him, "He's taken command. You've got to take charge. Press him harder."

Joe moved determinedly into the fifth round, firing that strong, straight left jab at his dancing foe and following up with rights to the body whenever he could get in close. Joe ducked under a long left by Conn and landed a hard left hook to the jaw that staggered Billy. The crowd came up screaming for the kill as Billy covered up, ducking and avoiding a rapid-fire flurry of blows by the champ. Billy was cut over the right eye before the bell rang. And in the sixth, he was cut over the nose as Joe jarred him with half a dozen different blows. After six rounds, Louis had won four on all three official scorecards and seemed well on his way to winning. The crowd was ready for the dynamite in his fists to explode.

But as Conn later commented, "I felt I'd tasted some of Joe's best blows and I was still standing. I wasn't surprised, but now I was sure I could take his best. I felt I could win if I went to work. I felt I had to take some chances to punch harder and hurt him more. I felt I could outbox him, but I had to hurt him more to take something out of him and slow him down and ease the pressure on me. I really went to work in the seventh." He moved dazzlingly. He began to throw more punches. Most landed. Louis did not land many. He landed his left jab and a few left hooks, but Billy ducked under rights. Joe boxed well and was not badly outboxed, but he was outboxed in the seventh, eighth, and ninth rounds.

All in the Polo Grounds were surprised and a lot of the fans started to holler for Billy, many thinking of him as "a great white hope." In the ninth, the cocky Conn was heard by ringsiders to say to Louis, "You got a tough fight tonight." Always a man of few words, Joe just said, "That's right." He knew it by then. Everyone knew it by then. Joe said later, "Conn was like a mosquito. He'd sting and flit away. I kept after him, but I couldn't catch him. I kept waiting for him to make a mistake." Billy said, "I wasn't thinking about making mistakes. I was thinking about winning. I was thinking I was going to win and I was sort of surprised." Everyone was, and there was bedlam in the ballpark by then.

In the tenth round Louis pressed, desperate for a knockout punch. He hit Conn hard, but was hit hard in return. Conn stood and traded punches with Louis, giving as well as he took, and this excited everyone. Conn was outboxing Louis and punching with him through the 11th and 12th rounds and becoming more confident every minute.

His cuts were repaired between rounds and weren't bothering him. In the 12th round a right cut him over the left eye, but it wasn't bad enough to bother him. He said, "I could see Joe was tiring and I thought I could knock him down if I could land a couple of hard punches. I figured I was ahead, but I wanted to win big and went for the knockout."

Louis said later, "I was tired. I was exhausted. I'd trained down too hard and used up a lot of strength chasing him. I hadn't been hurt, but I'd been hit a lot. I thought maybe I was losing my title and I was worried. I was hoping he'd take some chances and make a mistake so I could turn it around with one punch."

Between the 12th and 13th rounds Blackburn told Joe, "You're losing on points. You got to knock him out." Joe *was* losing on points, and Conn looked like a winner as he came out for the 13th. A left hook hurt Joe. Billy had been bombing Joe at the bell ending the 12th. Now with the bell beginning the 13th, he went for the kill with more bombs. He moved right in on Joe and jarred him with a left and right to the head. Louis hooked a left, but Billy hooked one right back.

Everyone was standing and screaming in the big ballpark as the stunning upset took shape in that spotlighted ring. All Conn had to do was win one of the last three rounds to take the title, but Billy was brave and daring and wanted to do it big. Conn dug a left hook deep into Joe's body and then brought up a left hand to the face that shook Louis. Louis blocked a left hook and hooked two lefts of his own and a straight right to the head that shook Conn.

Conn was courageous, but cut under the left eye by the last blow. He could taste the blood that dripped into his mouth. Angrily, he started to hook with his left. Joe moved inside it and fired a right hand right over it, right to Conn's jaw. It landed a little high, but it hurt Billy. Less than a minute was left in the round, but Louis saw his chance. Instead of moving away, Conn was standing, trying to battle back.

The perfect finisher, Louis stepped in with another right to the jaw, jarring Billy and making his legs buckle. Joe hooked a left that all but tore Conn's head off, then followed with a straight right to the chin that knocked Conn senseless. He fell flat on his back and lay twitching as ten was counted over him by the referee with only two seconds to go in the round.

It was all over at two minutes and 58 seconds of the 13th round. All Louis ever needed was an opening. The reckless Conn had given it to him. Now the fans were

Joe Louis's lethal left jab bends in nose of Billy Conn during spectacular comeback in their classic contest in June of 1941.

standing and cheering Joe. Now, wearily, Louis allowed his arm to be raised in triumph by announcer Harry Balogh. He watched as aides worked on Conn and helped him to his feet.

Louis said, "I felt like I'd gotten away with one. It was tough, the toughest. But I beat him. Billy made a mistake and that was all I ever needed to beat anyone."

He was cheered as he left the ring, covered with his hooded robe, and walked slowly down the aisle back to his dressing room beyond the dugout, still the champ. But Billy, too, was cheered as he left, grinning in crooked disappointment, his face cut and bruised after a fight, never to be forgotten, fought and lost and finished.

In his dressing room, Conn sat on a table while they dressed his wounds. He smiled wistfully and said, "I guess I got too much Irish in me. I lost my head. You can't trade punches with that man. Not all night. I had him on the hook and I let him get away. I was OK, though, wasn't I? I fooled a lot of people, didn't I? He's a helluva fighter, but I did everything but beat him, didn't I? I wish I was champ. Jeez, I wish I'd won that title. It would've been nice to win that thing. Aw, well, maybe I'll get another chance."

He did, but it came five years later and it was too late. World War II came along and dragged both fighters into service, and efforts to rematch them in a two-million-dollar match failed until five years later when Louis led all the way and easily knocked out Conn in the eighth. Louis always won his rematches. He had a dozen and he won them all, each one more easily than the first one. Of course, he won all but one of his fights—and that one was reversed in a rematch—until he retired with the crown after a record reign of almost 12 years and a record run of 25 straight successful defenses of his title. His fights with Conn and Gentleman Jim Braddock and Jersey Joe Walcott and his blitz of the Nazi, Schmeling, on the eve of the war with Germany are considered classics which the disappointment of his comeback cannot diminish.

Unlike the reluctant dragons of these days, Louis was fighting four foes a year when war came. If he had not been called into service, he might successfully have defended his title 10 or 12 more times during the first half of the 40s. As it was, he won 68 of 71 fights in a career that spanned 18 spectacular years in the ring as a professional fighter. He knocked out 55 foes with the most explosive punches in ring history. He performed from coast to coast across the country and boxed hundreds of exhibition matches here and elsewhere around the world.

Joe Louis came along at a time when there had been no black heavyweight champion since the "disgraced" Jack Johnson. Louis broke through the barriers of racial prejudice and helped open professional sports to blacks. He was idolized by the black community, but came to be equally popular with whites. He was simple and humble, yet bright and brilliant. He towered above all other athletes of his time. He became a folk figure of timeless stature, well-remembered, beloved, and honored into the 80s, revered by many who had not even been born when he finished fighting.

It's true that he always liked the good life. He liked the ladies and gambling on golf, and he spent his money until there was no more in a day when a dollar was worth several times what it is today. But he was a man of good will who never hurt anyone except those poor fellows he fought in the ring. Long after he'd retired, he used to spend all day in bed so he'd be fresh to party away the nights. I interviewed him many times and remember best the time, not too many years ago, when he received me propped up in bed during a day spent watching game shows on television. We talked about the good old days and he smiled broadly. "Hey, my day may be done, but I had me a heck of a lot of good days along the way. And some pretty good nights," he added.

Let's talk about them.

2

THE HARD YEARS

Joseph Louis Barrow was born on the 13th of May, 1914. His birthplace is listed as Lafayette, Alabama, but actually he was born at home on a farm between Lafayette and Cusseta in the Buckelaw Mountains of Chambers County. A midwife delivered him while all of the family but his mother were working in the fields. He is remembered as a big baby of about ten pounds.

His grandparents had been plantation slaves. His father's parents, the Harps, were owned by a wealthy white man, James Barrow, and Joe's father, Munrow, took his name. It is not clear whether Munrow was Barrow's son. Many slaves were given the names of their owners in those days. Munrow Barrow married Lily Reese and they had eight children—Susie, Lonnie, Eulalia, Emmarell, DeLeon, Alvanius, Joseph, and Vunice. Joe was the seventh and he was named after his father's brother-in-law, Joe Louis Nichols. Later, Joe used his first and middle names, Joe Louis, when he began to box.

Joe remembered that his father's mother had Cherokee Indian blood, but it is not clear whether she was full-blooded or half-blooded. There also was white as well as black blood in his background. There was not a lot of intermarriage between whites and blacks, but it was common for babies to be born out of wedlock to white and black parents. Joe has said, "I was mostly black. My family looked black and was black. A lot of people tried to pass themselves off as white or even Indian because they had some of that in their blood, but I was always proud to be black, a Negro."

There were as many poor whites as poor blacks (called Negroes in those days) in Chambers County, and there was segregation—the whites and blacks went to different schools and churches, for example—but there was little trouble between them. White and black children played together without trouble. A few whites had most of the money, but Joe played with the children of the white family which ran the general store and owned a lot of the land.

Joe recalls, "I guess we got along with the whites because we kept in our place, but there wasn't bad feelings between whites and black in the country like in the city. I didn't know about bad feelings till I got to the city. We didn't know the difference between blacks and whites in the country because most everyone farmed and worked hard and was poor in the country. We didn't know the difference between rich and poor because no one had nothing. All we knew was country and the life we led there and we didn't know how hard it was because we didn't see an easier side of life. All we knew was country."

Life was hard in that part of the country. The Barrow family was one of many digging a meager living out of the hard red clay earth. They planted, picked, and sold cotton, carting it to the town of Camp Hill. Everyone in a family worked the fields from sunup to sundown, in the humid heat and damp cold of Alabama's summers and winters. Girls worked as well as boys, young and old alike. Joe's mother, a large woman, worked almost a full day, leaving maybe an hour early to go home to fix supper for the family. She washed clothes at night, and got up an hour early to fix breakfast, and lunch for later.

"Mamas was special," Joe remembered. "They worked harder than anyone. Mine did. Mine was special. I knew it. At least I knew I'd do almost anything for a smile from her. She always said I was the worst crybaby of the bunch. She always said I howled the loudest when she took a stick to me for running out on my chores. But sometimes when I'd scrub the floors and she'd pick me up and give me a big kiss I was in heaven. I never really knew my father. I got a stepfather was the only father I really knew. My mama really raised me. She saw we went to church. She saw we did right. She was a good woman, tried to make us good."

Joe's father had gotten a 120-acre farm to work as a sharecropper. A large part of the earnings went to the landowner. The family that worked the land kept a share.

That was common in those days. The hard work was too much for Joe's father. He was more than six feet tall and about 200 pounds, but he broke down and was committed to the Searcy Hospital for the Negro Insane in nearby Mount Vernon when Joe was only two. The poor man escaped a few times and returned to live with his family for months at a time—for two years, one time—but there came a time when Joe was yet young when his mother was told that the father had died at the hospital, and she just accepted that. Later it turned out that the father was almost 60 before he died, but he never knew anything about his son's spectacular ring career.

With her husband gone, Lily Barrow had to work harder than ever to see that her family made it in the fields and had food on the table and clothes on their backs. What were considered good clothes were saved for Sundays and church. The kids wore patched overalls. They did not wear shoes. Neighboring families with men at the head of them helped out, as poor as they were, paying pennies to the Barrow kids for running errands or doing chores, sending over some extra food when they had any.

Joe remembers having had enough to eat—pork chops and chicken, potatoes and corn, mostly from their farm or neighbors' farms. He had so many pork chops, he wouldn't eat another one after he went out into the world. But he never lost his taste for chicken. Before he was big enough to work in the fields, his job was to take out to the family in the field the basket of food for lunch his mother had prepared that morning and kept in the shade. If there was chicken in it he sometimes ate it on the way, which got him whippings.

Their house was made of plain, unpainted wood—one room, a shack really. There was a wood stove for cooking and for heat. Lighting was by kerosene lamps, which were dim and smelled bad. There was no running water; water had to be brought in by bucket. There was no plumbing; there was an outhouse out back for a toilet. Inside, the beds were jammed together. The children slept two or three to a bed. Joe remembers hating it when he had to move over to make room for another. He remembers how crowded their family of nine or ten was. He used to like to go out in the woods to be by himself.

His mother's uncle, Peter Sheley, was sort of the man of the family, running the farm for a while. But when Joe was six, his mother married Patrick Brooks, a widower with eight children of his own. They moved with their 16 kids into a larger house on the Walton plantation near Waverly, a little deeper into the hills. The kids were thrown together and Joe remembers his stepfather as a fair man who treated them all alike. One of his stepfather's sons, Pat, was about the same age as Joe and they became special pals, but Joe remained a bit of a loner. Although their new, wooden house was larger, their family had doubled and the Barrows were more crowded than ever. The house had no more modern conveniences than the other one. Their life remained simple, primitive.

Patrick Brooks was also a sharecropper, and the combined families continued to work hard in the fields. Joe admits he was not a hard-working boy. He preferred playing games like "skin the tree," which was a sort of hide-and-seek in which one child would try to find the others and shake them out of the trees in which they hid. He went fishing and brought home fish for food. He had little interest in reading, writing, and arithmetic, and went to school only when he had to. Bigger than other kids his age and slower in his studies, he was teased a lot. He developed a stammer. He played hookey a lot, hunting snakes in the woods or lying in the grass and trying to figure out what the cloud formations looked like.

He hated the one-room schoolhouse at the Mt. Sinai Baptist Church and School, where there was one teacher for all the area's black children aged seven to seventeen. He didn't do well and hated the teacher, who made fun of him for not doing well. He was "left back" a few times and his younger sister caught him and passed him. No one seemed to care too much. He was going to be a farmer, anyway. What else was there?

He once said that he didn't think about it a lot. This simple, primitive, poor farm life was all he knew. As it turned out, he was smart enough, with a sort of natural wisdom. It didn't bother him that he didn't get a good education, or that he was slower in his studies than others, or that he was considered dumb. "One thing I learned was that it didn't take a lot of words to say what you had to say," he once said. All his life he said what he had to say in as few words as possible.

As long as he had food to eat, a bed to sleep in, a place to play, Joe was satisfied, but his parents were not. Some of the older children were marrying and having babies and the house was becoming more and more crowded, food and beds more and more scarce. Years the weather was bad, the crops were bad and it was a struggle just to survive.

Relatives returned from the north with tall tales of good jobs for big money in the factories. They didn't want to admit they had gone north and found life tough there too. They didn't want to admit that life in the black ghettos of the big cities up north could be as harsh in its own way as on the farms down south.

The thought of weekly paychecks appealed to Patrick Brooks and his older sons. The thought of life in the big city with electric lights and indoor bathrooms appealed to them all.

Patrick Brooks determined to go to Detroit to work in the automobile factories. He went, taking his wife and the older boys with him. Joe's uncle moved in to take care of the younger children left behind. Joe remembers the months he waited for the rest of the family to be called north as a long, lonely time. He knew nothing about Detroit, except it was a big city. He was not sure he wanted to go, but he had no choice. He was just 12 years old when the money came. An older sister bought new clothes and shoes for them and, riding a train for the first time in their lives, they went north to rejoin the rest of their family.

They moved in with relatives in a small house on MacCombs Street on the east side of Detroit. Soon they moved into their own place in a tenement on Catherine Street. They had electric lights, running water, and indoor plumbing. Joe recalls what a thrill it was just pulling a chain that flushed the toilet. They also saw how much better most whites lived in other parts of town. But for the first time they had a little money. Brooks had found work with the city as a street cleaner and the older boys had found work with Ford and other automotive plants.

Joe got city clothes—shorts and knickers, which were worn then, in the middle 1920s—but he was still a country boy. He did not feel at home in the city streets. He did make a few friends. He started to run with a sharpie, Freddie Guinyard, he met at the Calvary Baptist Church. As they grew up, they hauled vegetables and delivered groceries for the Eastern Market. They worked on ice wagons—skinny Freddie handled the horse while big Joe hauled the ice up flights of stairs to families without refrigerators. Joe didn't mind. He was happy to have a buddy. They spent all day Saturdays watching cowboy movies at the first theater Joe ever saw. If they went early, they got in for a nickel.

School was tough for Joe. He was behind the others and was put in with younger, smaller kids at the Duffield School. He couldn't catch up. He didn't try. He sat and stared out the window. He didn't cause any trouble; he was silent most of the time. The teachers sympathized with him. One, Vada Schwader, suggested he try a vocational school. She didn't know what she was saying when she said, "He's going to have to make a living with his hands. He'd better start now." He was sent to the Bronson Trade School, where he learned to make tables, chairs, and cabinets. Some of these things he got to take home and they helped furnish his family's small, crowded place. He liked this school a little better.

But the Depression developed then, in the early 1930s. Auto sales fell off. Workers were laid off. One by one, Joe's stepfather and older brothers lost their jobs. They went on relief, but there wasn't enough money to go around. Food was hard to come by and Joe's mother used to stand in line for handouts offered by the government. Joe remembered, "We'd had hard times before, but for the first time there were times we were hungry. You couldn't go pick some food out of the fields in Detroit."

Detroit was full of blacks from the South who had come north to make money and now were going hungry. There were a lot of whites selling apples on street corners across the country, but the blacks were the first to be fired and the last to be hired. There were a lot of bitter, disappointed black families in the north and their kids were ready to riot. Joe started to run with a gang of bitter black kids on Catherine Street. He was bigger than most and stronger and, when put to a test, it turned out that he was pretty fair with his fists.

His mother worried desperately that he was going to get into trouble. As scarce as money was, she scraped up 50 cents a week to send him to a violin teacher on Woodward Avenue. She scraped up a few dollars to rent him a violin. Somehow, she thought he could be saved if he could make music a career. He hated it. He didn't do well with the lessons. He hated carrying the violin to school. The other kids kidded him. All Joe could do was punch them.

There was one kid, Thurston McKinney, who did not tease Joe. McKinney was a school hero because he had won a Golden Gloves title in Detroit, boxing at 147 pounds. He thought Joe, too, might make it as a fighter, and persuaded him to go to the Brewster Recreation Center to try out. Joe had been sparring in his backyard with a buddy, Amsey Rinson, and talking about trying out as a fighter. One day, instead of going for his music lesson, Joe went to the gym. He took his mama's 50 cents for a music lesson, rented a locker, and put his violin in it.

For a while then, Joe took the money his mama gave him for music and used it for the gym. The violin lessons only lasted a month or so, but his mama didn't know for a long time. McKinney lent Joe trunks and tennis shoes and Joe returned the violin and bought boxing gloves with the money. When the violin teacher told his mother he had stopped, she was disappointed. But when the teacher told her he had no talent for the violin and Joe told her how good he was at boxing, she said she'd help him with money for that.

Joe loved the gym. He loved hitting the light bag and the heavy bag and getting to work out in the ring with his hero, McKinney, who was only a year or so older than he. He and McKinney and Rinson became buddies, working out at the gym every chance they could. Atler Ellis, who operated the gym, was impressed with Joe. He offered to teach Joe if he would train regularly. Joe was thrilled; he had found something he could do.

Ellis taught Joe how to move his feet, hold his hands, block and duck punches, throw a left jab, a left hook, a straight right. A six-footer who weighed 170 pounds, Joe learned fast. These were lessons he could deal with. And he had things that could not be taught—fast hands and punching power.

No one knows why some men hit harder than others. Joe was a big kid, but some skinny fellows have been much harder hitters than some muscular men. Whatever it was, Joe had it. He had not only a good build for a boxer and strength, but punching power. The smaller McKinney stopped sparring with him after Joe staggered him and almost put him down with a punch. Joe put bigger guys down.

His reputation grew rapidly around the area. Joe loved it. He became a hero to the younger kids in the neighborhood, even though he'd not yet had a fight. One, Walker Smith, used to carry his gym bag just to get to go to the gym with Joe and watch him work out. Walker Smith later became a boxer, too. He adopted another name so he could begin before he was 18 and of age. He became known as "Sugar" Ray Robinson.

At 17, in 1932, Joe Louis Barrow quit school to try to become a boxer. He hustled up any kind of job he could find to make a dollar during the day, and worked out at the gym every night. He was happy. "I believe in education now," he once told me, "but I wasn't going anywhere in school then. I thought I could get somewhere in the ring. My mama didn't think so. My stepfather didn't think so. They wanted me to get a steady job. But all I wanted was to be a boxer. It was like I'd found religion."

LEARNING TO BOX

Joe Louis Barrow quit school early in 1932 before he turned 18. He found a part-time job for twenty dollars a week pushing truck bodies to the paint sprayer along the assembly line at the Briggs Auto Body plant. When he worked, he worked eight to five with an hour off for lunch. It was hard work and his back ached at the end of the day.

He wanted to be a boxer, but he was so tired at the end of the day that he often didn't go to the gym. Most of his training took place on his Saturdays off. Atler Ellis got Holman Williams, a working middleweight, to work with Joe. Louis recalled, "Williams was a beautiful boxer. He taught me a lot and encouraged me a lot."

Although Joe's mother hadn't said he couldn't box, he knew she didn't expect him to make a living at it. His stepfather figured a steady job was the only way to make a living. Joe brought his buddy, Thurston McKinney, home to explain to the old man that Joe could get merchandise checks worth five to twenty-five dollars just for fighting as an amateur. Mr. Brooks liked that.

Nevertheless, when Joe applied for an amateur license, he used the name Joe Louis. He figured some of the fight results might wind up in the newspapers and he wasn't sure he wanted his mother or stepfather to know. He never went back to his full name.

Louis fought his first fight as an amateur at the Naval Armory in November of 1932 at the age of 18. Atler Ellis arranged a bout with Johnny Miller, who had been on the U.S. Olympic team in the Games in Los Angeles that year. He was too experienced and skilled for Joe. Holman Williams saw that and argued against it. But Ellis thought Joe hit too hard for his foe. Joe himself didn't know the difference; he thought he could beat almost anybody. Until he fought Miller.

Louis never reached Miller. The veteran amateur knocked him down seven times and stopped him in two rounds. Joe's first fight was a fiasco. He was beaten up pretty badly. When he went home, his stepfather took one look at Joe's face and laughed. His mother saw him and cried. Joe was discouraged. He didn't go back to the gym for several months. He found a full-time job at the Ford factory at River Rouge for a steady twenty-five dollars a week. Now he was pushing truck bodies around. It was back-breaking work.

He had a girl friend he never forgot, Bennie Franklin. She was stepdaughter to one of Joe's sisters. Although there was no blood between them, they figured the family wouldn't approve. They sneaked around, dating at amusement parks and movies. They had picnics. They went to Belle Island, a well-liked place located between Michigan and Ontario, Canada. They went together from the time Joe was 14 until he left Detroit at 20.

Joe wanted more money to take her places. He wanted more money, period. He started to think again about boxing professionally. "I figured if I could make seventy, seventy-five bucks a week I'd be happy," he once said, laughing. There would come a time when he'd make hundreds of thousands of dollars a minute. He figured if he was going to be too tired at the end of the workday to take his girl friend out, what was the point of working?

His friends, Freddie Guinyard, Amsey Rinson, Thurston McKinney, and his stepbrother Pat Brooks, teased him about the beating he'd taken and about his having given up. He wanted to prove them wrong about his ability to box. He wanted to prove to his stepfather that he could box. Holman Williams kept after him to give it another try. Joe figured boxing was better than working for a living.

There were two times in his career when Louis might have given up the game or never made it to the top. One came later when he was beaten badly and stopped by the German, Max Schmeling. Many fighters never recover their confidence from a loss like that and fail to become the boxers they might be, but Louis bounced back to take the title and avenge the defeat. The other came when he was beaten badly and stopped by his first amateur foe, and stopped going to the gym. But Joe left Ford in January of 1933 and returned to the ring.

Williams worked with Joe. Atler Ellis worked with Joe. One time, Atler tied Joe's right hand to a ring post and made him box Thurston McKinney with his left hand so Joe would learn to use his left better. Joe learned a little, but he was immobilized and beaten up. Louis didn't think much of Ellis's training techniques. Neither did Williams. He never had forgiven Ellis for matching Joe in his first fight against an experienced foe.

Williams set up Joe's second fight, against Otis Thomas at the Forest Athletic Club in Detroit. This was in February of 1933. Louis knocked out Thomas with two punches, a left hook and a straight right to the jaw, in the first round. Louis took his $25 winner's merchandise check home. "It was one of the thrills of my life," he recalled later.

Williams found fighters Louis could deal with. Joe knocked out 14 foes in a row, gaining confidence in himself as he went. He took some of his $25 merchandise checks home, pleasing his stepfather. Joe bought things with others, sold others. His mother and sisters slipped him money. Williams slipped him money. Joe got by.

Williams saw that Louis was ready to make a move. He wanted him to enter the Golden Gloves boxing tournament and go against the best amateurs in the Detroit area and maybe go against the best in the country in competition with the best in other cities. Williams himself was moving up in the middleweight ranks as a pro and didn't have time to take on a fighter full time. He would become one of the best, though he never took a title. He didn't trust Atler Ellis to move Joe with caution. He took Joe to the Detroit Athletic Club, where George Slayton was the boss. Slayton began to work with the youngster.

Louis saw little of friends. He worked hard. His coach moved him around the country. He may have moved him too fast. Joe was outpointed by Clint Bridges in Chicago and Max Marek in Detroit. Both were bigger and more experienced than the 19-year-old, 170-pound Louis. Louis won six fights in a row in the National Amateur Championships, but lost the light-heavyweight title bout to Marek, a football star at Notre Dame. Louis's fourth and last defeat as an amateur came to another bigger and more experienced fighter, Stanley Evans, in Detroit. But Louis defeated Evans in a rematch later to win the light-heavyweight title in the Detroit Golden Gloves tournament.

Afterward, Slayton brought John Roxborough to the dressing room to meet Joe. This was the turning point in Joe's career. Black fighters had a tough time in the ring in those days. They couldn't get wealthy whites to back them. But Roxborough was a wealthy black. He was a powerful figure in the numbers racket in Detroit. In the numbers game, you played a three-digit number—678, or something like that. You bet a few coins or a few dollars. If your number came in, you collected many times your wager. The daily number was the last three digits of the betting at the race track or the stock market at the end of the day. Poor people played the numbers. It didn't cost much and it was the stuff of dreams.

Although what he did was illegal, John Roxborough was respected by the poor blacks in Detroit. He made money off them, but they felt he did not cheat them. He took a lot of the money and spent it on poor blacks—some he sent to college. Roxborough had a real estate office. His brother was a lawyer and an influential figure in black politics. Both were members of the Urban League and Young Negro Progressive Association. Roxborough and his brother were respected members of the community. Although he had a bad background and criminal connections, Roxborough did right by Joe Louis and there never was any scandal connected to their association.

Roxborough was impressed by Joe's potential and offered to sponsor him. Joe was impressed by Roxborough's fine manner, fine clothes, fine home, and other evidence of money. Joe asked Roxborough to come home and talk to his mother. Roxborough did so and impressed Mrs. Barrow, who gave her blessing to the deal. John Roxborough took over the ring career of Joe Louis. He gave Joe money for new trunks, a robe, and his first pair of boxing shoes. Until then Joe had been wearing sneakers. He saw to it that Joe had clean tape and bandages for every bout. He even gave Joe some of his old ties, shirts, and suits, which were altered to fit the youngster. He gave Joe five or ten bucks a week pocket money.

Louis had his last amateur fight in Ford Field, Detroit, in June of 1934. He knocked out Joe Bauer midway through the first round in an intracity match with the Cleveland Golden Gloves champions. That gave Joe 43 knockouts and 50 victories in 54 amateur bouts. Roxborough was anxious to turn Joe pro. That same month he took Joe to Chicago to introduce him to his new co-manager, Julian Black.

Louis was confused. He had thought Roxborough could do anything for him that had to be done. What he did not know was that Black, another numbers operator, had bailed Roxborough out of financial troubles earlier. Black asked Roxborough to repay the debt with half of Joe's contract. Black had connections in the boxing business and a stable of black fighters in Chicago. He could do a lot for Joe that his partner could not do. He assured Joe that he would take care of him. He did, too. As co-managers, neither Roxborough nor Black ever involved Joe in shady dealings.

The best thing Black did for Joe was to bring in Jack Blackburn as his trainer. Blackburn was a skinny, gaunt-looking guy. He had a nasty-looking scar running along his left cheek from his mouth to his ear. He had a nasty reputation, having served five years in prison for killing a man in a knife fight in his youth. But he had come out to become a brilliant lightweight fighter, though never a champion. After retiring in 1923, he took to training and developed two world champions, bantamweight Bud Taylor and lightweight Sammy Mandell.

Blackburn was an even better teacher than he had been a fighter. He saw Joe's power and potential from the first day in the gym, but he also saw flaws in Joe's style that had not been corrected by previous teachers. For example, Joe often was off-balance when he punched. Joe was taught how to plant his feet and get his body behind his punches. He was taught to really drive the left jab so it became one of boxing's classic punches. Because he was not fast on his feet, Joe was taught the relentless shuffling-forward style of offense that became his trademark.

In his successful career as an amateur, Joe had gained a lot of confidence in his future as a fighter. However, he was surprised at how fast he improved under Blackburn in four weeks of hard work before he even had his first professional fight. Blackburn introduced Joe to roadwork and got him to running six miles a morning around Washington Park. Then he worked him hard shadowboxing, hitting the light and heavy bags, and sparring with different types of foes several hours a day in George Trafton's gym.

Blackburn warned Joe that black fighters had to be better than white fighters to get ahead in the game. This was the 1930s, and there was much more racial discrimination in this country than there is today. The southern part of this country practiced segregation. So, for that matter, though to a lesser degree, did the northern part. Blacks could use the same drinking fountains and rest rooms as whites in the north, but they were not welcome everywhere. Blacks had not yet broken through the racial barriers in big league baseball or other sports. There were and had been a few black boxing champions, but none in the heavyweight ranks since Jack Johnson held the title from 1910 through 1915. A high-living man who ran with white women, Johnson supposedly disgraced blacks and the title. However, a white who lived a similar life style would not have come into nearly so much criticism.

Blackburn, who had trained two whites to titles, thought Louis could become the next black titleholder in the heavyweight ranks. There were not a lot of good fighters in the heavyweight ranks at the time. But Blackburn warned Joe that he might lose a lot of doubtful decisions if he let his fights go to the finish. He warned Joe that the surest way to defeat a white foe was to knock him out. Fortunately, Joe had the ability to do so. He had an awesome punch with either hand. But the easygoing youngster had to be made mean. He would always be easygoing outside the ring, but he came to be mean inside the ring.

Blackburn wouldn't let Joe let up on a foe even in the training ring. As a result, despite the heavily padded gloves and headgear the fighters wore while sparring in the gym, Joe frequently floored foes. No one ever sparred harder. It became a problem for Blackburn to find sparring partners willing to work with Joe. Eventually he found George Nicholson, who was willing to take the punishment. He was well-paid and became well-known as Joe's main sparring partner. After Joe became a champ, large crowds paid just to see him work out, mainly because his workouts were so much fiercer than those of other champs.

Blackburn worked especially hard with Joe on finishing off foes. If Joe hit them right, he could knock them out with one punch, which is really rare. If he didn't, he hurt them. The thing then was to take advantage of this chance to finish off a hurt fighter. Most young fighters flail away wildly in their impatience to put their foes down. More of their punches may miss than land, and their hurt foe gets a chance to recover. Blackburn taught Joe to take his time, to move right in on a hurt foe, to concentrate on landing hard, accurate blows.

Although slow-footed, Joe became a good boxer. He still made mistakes Blackburn never could correct completely. He was hit with good punches from time to time and hurt by them and even knocked down by them. But Joe was strong and determined and was able to shake off the effects of such blows and go on to win. He had fast hands and no one ever hit harder. But, as much as his ability to hurt foes, it was his ability to finish off foes that made him a great fighter, maybe the greatest ever. And, among other things, Blackburn brought that to Joe.

The two black men—the one short, thin, and mean-looking, the other tall, husky, and pleasant-looking, the one 40 and the other 20—took to each other right away. Blackburn called Joe "Chappie," so Joe called Jack "Chappie" right back. As Joe's trainer, "Chappie" became almost as famous as Joe. Joe always gave him credit for his success. Joe later said, "Chappie did more for my fighting than any other man. I wanted to learn and he taught me. I trusted him as I never trusted any other man. He made me a champion." Blackburn said, "Joe did it, not me. I helped, but he had the ability. A lot of young guys won't listen. Joe listened. It was a team thing."

So, midway through 1934, the team that would scale the heavyweight heights was set—Joe doing the fighting, Blackburn the training, and Roxborough and Black managing the effort.

Black became the main money man, though Roxborough continued to exert a lot of influence. Joe was provided a place to live, clothes, expenses, and walking-around money. While their deal with Joe called for his managers to take half his earnings, they let Joe keep all of his small early purses and encouraged him to send money home. He was moved into an apartment on East 46th Street in Chicago with a good-natured guy named Bill Bottoms. A chef by trade, Bottoms would cook for Louis the rest of his career. He got Joe off hot dogs and apple pie and onto steak and vegetables. Originally assigned also to chaperone Joe, Bottoms became his friend and confidant. When Joe got lonely in Chicago and homesick for Detroit, Black brought in Joe's old buddy,

Freddie Guinyard, to move in with Joe and be his buddy. Black didn't miss a trick. He had a lot at stake in his hot prospect.

Boxing was bigger in those days than it is today. Baseball was the big game, but professional football, basketball, and hockey were not nearly what they are today. Ring kings like Barney Ross and Kid Chocolate were real heroes. But, traditionally, boxing attracts the most attention when there is an outstanding heavyweight champion setting the pace for the rest, and there was not one at that time. Max Baer had just become champ by knocking out Primo Carnera. But it was a one-sided fight which exposed Carnera as a fraud, a giant promoted to prominence by mobsters. No one knew how good Baer was. He had ability, but lacked dedication. He was better known as a clown than as a boxer. Jack Dempsey and Gene Tunney had been retired since the end of the 1920s and the sporting world was hungry for a heavyweight champion who excited the fans.

As an amateur, Joe Louis had attracted the sort of attention Cassius Clay would draw years later when he turned pro and before he became Muhammad Ali. The sporting public was watching in the mid-1930s when the highly touted young Negro knockout artist from Detroit turned pro in Chicago.

TURNING PRO

Because of his prominence as an amateur, Joe Louis's first fight as a professional was a main event. In fact, he never fought less than a main event in his professional career. His first fight was scheduled as a 10-rounder. Some of his other fights his first year were scheduled at eight or six rounds, but his bouts always received top billing.

Since he never had gone more than three rounds as an amateur, Joe was concerned about having to go 10 in his first fight as a pro. Blackburn assured Joe that he could knock out his first foe in a round or two, and that he would seldom have to go more than three or four rounds in his early bouts.

As it turned out, Joe had to go 10 full rounds or more only 10 times in more than 60 fights before he retired with the title. In 71 professional fights, he KO'd 54 foes, 10 in the first round, 10 in the second, and 12 in the third.

He KO'd his first foe in the first round. This was Jack Kracken on the Fourth of July, 1934, at the Bacon Casino on the south side of Chicago. Kracken was a local light-heavyweight with a little experience. Joe was inexperienced, but he was a heavyweight by this time, having grown past the 175-pound light-heavyweight limit to 181 pounds.

As Louis later recalled it, "I was scared. This was my first fight for real money. The other guy was white and looked like he'd been around. He looked confident in the ring. But Chappie told me not to worry. He told me to hit him in the belly until I brought his guard down, then go for the jaw. I did what he told me and it worked."

Louis laid into his older foe, working both hands to the stomach. When Kracken dropped his hands to protect his midsection, Louis landed a left hook to the chin and dropped his foe for the ten-count in less than two minutes. Joe jumped for joy and his pal, Guinyard, jumped into the ring to celebrate with him.

Back in the dressing room, Blackburn told Joe to take it easy. "You're gonna knock out a lot of guys before you're done. You can't get carried away with it every time. You got to take it in stride." Roxborough advised, "Don't show your emotions. They can't get to you if you don't give yourself away." Black added, "Do it with dignity."

Gradually, Louis developed the deadpan style which characterized his ring conduct. His face was expressionless in the ring. He didn't show joy or sorrow. He didn't smile and he didn't clown around.

Joe was paid $52 for his first fight as a pro. Roxborough gave him the check and told him to keep it all—

or rather, send it home to his mother. Joe sent $40 of it home. He kept 12 bucks to go bowling with his buddy and have some hot dogs and hamburgers. He was just 20 years old and he hadn't learned how to live it up with the ladies and all in high style. Unfortunately, that was something he would learn.

"I thought fifty-two bucks was a lot of loot for two minutes' work," Louis later laughed. "A few years later I was giving out fifties for tips."

His second pro bout, exactly one week later, was worth eight dollars more. Back at the Bacon Casino, he fought a friend from the gym, Willie Davis, and knocked him out in three rounds. Because he was the second foe and not the first, Davis is forgotten. But as Joe Louis's first victim, Jack Kracken is forever famous.

The end of July, Joe was booked into one of the main arenas in the area, Marigold Gardens. Joe KO'd Larry Udell in two. He sold out the place, so they brought him back two weeks later for another full house. Jack Kranz slipped Joe's best shots and went the six-round distance, but dropped a decision.

Two weeks later, near the end of August, Joe blasted Buck Everett in two. After five straight victories in Chicago, there was interest in Detroit for Joe to box in his home town.

The Detroit *Times* set up Joe's first fight as a professional in Detroit where he'd had his first fight as an amateur: the Naval Armory. Louis flattened Alex Borchuk of Canada in four. But Borchuk battled bravely and landed a blow to the jaw that chipped one of Joe's back teeth before going down.

Joe was paid only $106 for the fight and he'd been making closer to $200 a fight by then. And, he later reported, Bingo Brown, boss of the Michigan Boxing Commission, had called Roxborough to the office and tried to high-pressure him into taking on a white manager on the threat of being barred from boxing in that state.

"My man didn't back down, but the other guy did," Joe later recalled. "Wasn't long before I was too big to be kept out of my home town, anyway."

Joe blew his purse on bowling and burgers with his buddies before he returned to Chicago. Late in September, he took on Adolph Wiater at Arcadia Gardens. Wiater had defeated Johnny Risko, a ranking contender for heavyweight honors. He was smart and skilled. He avoided Joe's best punches and tied him up in repeated clinches. He respected the youth's punching ability so much, he didn't take any chances. He went 10, but Joe hit him enough to win the decision.

Joe was disappointed, but Blackburn told him, "Some men will go the distance with you 'cause that's all they want to do. If you win, that's all you got to do."

Louis received his top purse of $200 for the bout and a lesson from Blackburn on how to spin out of clinches and deal with opponents who stay tight and hang on a lot. His next fight, Louis got $280 for dealing with Art Sykes, another experienced performer. Louis had his hands full with Sykes, but took him out with a right to the head in the eighth round. It was such a powerful punch that Sykes was out for a long time. His handlers couldn't revive him, nor could a couple of doctors who entered the ring. He was taken to a hospital. It was a couple of hours before he came back to consciousness.

Louis said, "I was scared I'd killed him. I don't know if I coulda handled that. I think I might have quit." Luckily, he never killed a man in the ring, though others, such as Max Baer, the reigning heavyweight champion, did. When you are hitting a man in the head, you can hurt him. You are being hit and you can be hurt, too.

There are rules designed to protect fighters from serious injury and a referee in the ring to enforce the rules, but it is a dangerous sport. And Joe Louis rapidly was gaining a reputation as the kind of puncher who could hurt a man. In a way, it helped him. Many of his foes entered the ring too afraid of him to fight their best fight.

After only three months in the ring as a pro, Louis was beginning to meet better boxers. Less than a week after rendering Sykes unconscious, he returned to Detroit to KO Jack O'Dowd in two. About two weeks later he was booked back into the Arcadia Gardens in Chicago against Stan Poreda, a hot young heavyweight in the east, out of Hoboken, New Jersey. Joe took care of him in one round.

The end of November, after just ten fights, Louis was booked into the big building in town, Chicago Stadium, against Charley Massera, a highly touted young slugger from Monongahela, Pennsylvania. It was publicized as a slugfest between two of the best young knockout artists in boxing. It lasted three rounds and Joe flattened his foe. Joe picked up his first thousand-dollar purse—$1,100. But by then his managers were picking up their half.

About two weeks later, in mid-December, Louis was brought back to the Stadium to take on Lee Ramage of Los Angeles, who ranked in the top ten among heavyweights. Some thought Ramage would be too smart and durable for Louis. Ramage never had been knocked down. But Louis cornered him in the third, brought his guard down with a left to the stomach, and knocked him down and out with a right to the jaw. Joe was paid $2,500 and finished the year with a record of 12 straight triumphs, 10 by knockout.

After only six months as a pro, Joe was beginning to make a little money in a day when a dollar was worth three or four times what it is today. He had taken his family off the relief rolls and had repaid relief authorities $270 they had given his family. He had given gifts of cash and clothing to his parents, his brothers, and his sisters. He had given gifts and cash to friends. He was a soft touch for a loan.

Unfortunately, money never meant much to Joe. The more he got, the more he spent. It did not matter much while he was not making much, but as he began to make more and his expenses started to rise, he began to fall behind in paying his bills. Taxes were not heavy in the mid 1930s, but as taxes rose he began to fall behind in paying them. He always paid taxes, but the time came when it seemed he could not keep up.

If Roxborough and Black betrayed Joe in any way, it was that they did not provide the guidance he needed to hang onto his hard-earned money. They did not cheat Joe. They did not waste his money. They took their half and let him have his. In fact, they often advanced him money against his next purse when he ran short. But this became a bad habit of Joe's—asking for advances, spending his money before he made it.

It is not uncommon in boxing for managers to take half a fighter's earnings. Maybe this is too much, but often they support a fighter until he begins to make money and lose a lot of money on fighters who do not make it. They are responsible for making his matches, and if they do not develop him properly by advancing him gradually, and if they do not get him good deals when he is ready, they are not earning their money.

Joe never was selfish about money. He spent as much on others as on himself. But he did spend on himself. He liked flashy cars and bought his first car in 1934, a black Buick. He liked flashy clothes and bought his first suits, usually striped and with wide lapels. He liked broad-brimmed hats. He was becoming a bit of a fancy-dressed dude.

He liked the ladies and broke training to be with one before the Massera fight. He felt so guilty that he ran 12 miles instead of six the next morning and insisted on sparring six rounds instead of three that afternoon. Chappie couldn't figure out why Joe suddenly was so ambitious. "What's with you, boy?" he asked suspiciously. He soon knew what was going on. He kept after Joe to resist temptation. It became tougher and tougher. But Joe didn't drink and he trained hard.

Louis liked parties. Before the Ramage bout he met a young woman he really liked. After the bout he threw a party just so he could get together with her. She was Marva Trotter, an 18-year-old secretary who was taking courses at the University of Chicago and at a school of design. She admired his brawn and he admired her brains. Also, he thought she was beautiful.

She became his girl and eventually he married her.

After the Ramage bout, Roxborough and Black let Joe return to Detroit to spend the year-end holidays with his family and friends. Years later Joe recalled, "Must be the best Christmas we ever had. Had money for the first time and didn't mean nothing to spend it. I got gifts for everyone. Had me a good time with everyone. Everyone was sure I was going to be champ. So was I. I had no worries. I had a long way to go, but I knew I'd get there. Life was easy."

It would get tougher. By year's end he was anxious to get back to his new girl friend in Chicago. Blackburn was anxious to get him back in training for his first full year as a professional. Black and Roxborough were anxious to book some big-money bouts for the young fighter, who had become the sensation of the boxing world. But they were rebuffed by New York promoters. Not knowing they were black, one told them on the telephone, "I can help him here, but you know he can't win every time he goes in the ring. After all, he's a nigger."

"So am I," said Roxborough, who hung up on him.

Others offered less money than they would have given whites, less than Louis was worth. So the managers took their ring sensation on tour. Other cities in the country were as anxious to see Joe as New York was. Not all could afford big money, but Louis did not have to take on tough fighters at every stop.

Blackburn pleaded with the managers not to push the fighter too fast. He proved his point when Joe could not put away Patsy Perroni at Detroit's big building, the Olympia, the fourth of January in his first fight of 1935.

Out of Cleveland, Perroni had six years' experience in the ring. He was smart and rugged. Joe floored him three times, but Perroni kept getting up. Perroni could not floor Joe, but he shook him several times. Joe got the decision after 10 rounds and earned $4,200, within $500 of his first year's earnings. But he earned it. "He learned me a lot of lessons," Joe later admitted. "At least I proved I could take it."

One week later he was in Duquesne Gardens, Pittsburgh, earning every cent of a $1,900 purse against tough Hans Birkie, who taught Joe a few tricks while trying to last the distance with him, but was nailed and knocked out in the 10th and last round. Louis was learning his trade as he went.

Six weeks later, he landed in Los Angeles for a rematch outdoors at Wrigley Field with Lee Ramage and this time took him out in two rounds, earning his top purse of $4,300. In San Francisco he flattened Donald "Red" Barry in three rounds for $3,200.

California writers wrote glowingly of this spectacular youngster. Scotty Monteith, a veteran promoter, called him a "brown bomber" and the nickname caught on with the writers and was to stick to Joe from then on.

Far more than it is now, New York was the center of the sports scene. Until you made it in The Big City in boxing, you hadn't made it. And interest in "The Brown Bomber" was growing in New York. Sportswriters and fans wanted to see the sensation from the Midwest. James J. (Jimmy) Johnston promoted the fights at Madison Square Garden, the most glamorous indoor arena in the nation, and so had a corner on the big bouts put on outdoors at Yankee Stadium or the Polo Grounds. He wouldn't give Louis a shot unless he got control of the fighter. Johnston was known as "The Boy Bandit," although it had been a long time since he was a boy. He was tough to do business with.

Several promoters had tried to take over Johnston's territory, but "The Boy Bandit" had the best fighters tied up. The latest to try was Mike Jacobs, a Broadway character who had made a lot of money "scalping" show tickets—using connections to buy the best tickets to the hot shows and then selling them for five to ten times their face value when the shows were sold out.

Jacobs wanted to put on his own shows. He wasn't interested in musicals or dramas. He was interested in boxing. He was a hustler—smart, tough, ambitious—and he was looking for an angle with which he could cut into Jimmy Johnston's territory.

Jacobs's first break came when the two Hearst newspapers in town turned on Johnston for raising the rent every year on major bouts they sponsored at the Garden on behalf of the Free Milk Fund, their pet charity which provided milk for needy children. Jacobs got together with Ed Frayne, sports editor of the New York *American*, Bill Farnsworth, sports editor of the New York *Journal*, and Damon Runyon, the sports columnist who became famous for fiction about Broadway characters. Jacobs agreed to put on major ring shows for them cheaply in the name of charity. They agreed to back him in the formation of a new promotional organization, the 20th Century Sporting Club.

However, Jacobs had access to only a few of the top fighters and he could not get into the Garden without a fighter or fighters the head of the Garden, John Reed Kilpatrick, wanted more than those Johnston had.

The editor of the boxing magazine *Ring*, Nat Fleischer, had been touting this kid in the Midwest, Joe Louis, to Jacobs. But Jacobs was wary of black fighters. He had no prejudice against blacks—his only prejudice was in favor of money—but black fighters were harder to promote than white fighters. There hadn't been a black able to get the heavyweight title in 20 years. Although he was one of the great fighters of all time, Harry Wills had not even been able to get a shot at Jack Dempsey's title. However, when Jacobs went to Miami Beach to promote a bout between Barney Ross and Frankie Klick, Ross's managers Sam Pian and Art Winch, Chicagoans, also told Jacobs he was missing a bet if he didn't look into Louis, a black fighter who might be hard to hold back.

After Ross whipped Klick, Jacobs flew to Los Angeles to see Louis knock out Ramage. He was excited by what he saw. He saw in The Brown Bomber a knockout artist who could pump new life into the boxing game. He felt that if a public demand for Louis could be built up he would have to be given his chance despite his color. With the Hearst newspapers behind him, he thought he could build up that demand. If Louis was as good as he looked, the Garden would give in to Jacobs in order to get Louis. Jacobs suggested to Roxborough and Black they put Louis in with a good fighter in a big fight in Chicago or Detroit as a test and he would bring in the big boxing writers and columnists from the east to see what they thought.

Joe was booked against a ranked heavyweight, Natie Brown, at Detroit's Olympia the end of March. Jacobs reserved a special car on a train from New York and luxury rooms at the best hotel in Detroit for 25 or so of the top sportswriters. He wined them and dined them.

It might have been a mistake. Brown was smart, tough, and clever. Once he tasted Louis's punching power, Natie decided the best thing he could do was go the distance. He didn't fight with Joe, but tied him up, covered up. Joe shook him up and cut him up, but Natie, the cutie, went the distance. Joe took the 10-round decision, but many were unimpressed.

Fortunately the New York writers were not among those. Had they been, the buildup could have collapsed right then and there. But they knew boxing. They saw what Brown had to do just to stay alive against this strong youngster. They told Jacobs the kid could be a winner and sent back stories that The Brown Bomber was a kid who could take the title.

Following the fight, Jacobs met with Roxborough, Black, and Louis at their victory celebration at the Frog Club, a Negro night club in Detroit. When Louis said, "I'm sorry I didn't do better," Jacobs said, "Forget it, kid, you did fine." He told the three that if they would throw in with him he would do his best to take over New York for them. They asked him what he wanted in return, how big a piece of Joe? He told them he didn't want to cut into their contract; he only wanted the rights to promote Joe's major fights. They were surprised and pleased.

Jacobs went to the men's room while they talked it

over. The co-managers told Joe they needed a New York promoter like Mike to break into the big time. Joe said OK. They joined Jacobs in the men's room. Here, where the noisy celebration could not be heard, Jacobs pulled out a contract calling for exclusive rights to promote Joe's fights. The three signed.

It was a major moment in the history of boxing. If Jacobs did not deliver the right fights for Louis, Joe's career would inevitably be curtailed. If Joe could not deliver in the fights, Jacobs' career would be curtailed.

As it turned out, however, both delivered. Promoter Jacobs joined co-managers Roxborough and Black, trainer Blackburn, and fighter Louis as the fifth and final piece that completed the puzzle of how to get a black fighter to the top in boxing.

This was long before blacks like Floyd Patterson, Sonny Liston, George Foreman, Joe Frazier, and Muhammad Ali came to dominate the heavyweight title. Had it not been for Joe Louis, they might never have had the chance.

While Jacobs returned to New York to set up Louis's debut in The Big Town, Roxborough and Black took Louis back on tour. He had made his top purse, $6,500, for the Brown bout, and he picked up much more, $11,000, for a third-round knockout of Roy Lazer in Chicago two weeks later.

He settled for a thousand or so here and there as he knocked out Biff Benton in two in Dayton, Roscoe Toles

A young Joe Louis watches hungrily and affectionately as his mother, Lily Barrow Brooks, fries chicken after her arrival at his Chicago apartment in 1937.

in six in Flint, Willie Davis in two in Peoria, and Gene Stanton in three in Kalamazoo.

Joe got a friend to help him pick out a house for his mother, and on Easter Sunday, 1935, he surprised her with a two-story, four-bedroom place at 2100 McDougal Avenue in Detroit. It cost him $9,000, plus $2,500 for repairs and $3,000 for furnishings.

A little later he also bought her a chicken ranch outside of town. Stepfather Patrick Brooks suddenly was saying nothing about boxing being a bad way to earn a living.

Joe also made down payments on houses for his sisters Susie and Emmarell in Detroit and stepbrother Pat Brooks in Wayne. He wanted everyone to be as happy as he was. Spending money made him happy.

By mid-May, 1935, when he turned 21, Joe Louis was just beginning to make big money in boxing. In less than a year of fighting professionally he'd won 22 straight bouts, 18 by knockout. He now topped 190 pounds and his management regarded him as ready to beat the best in the heavyweight ranks. And the boxing world was waiting to see him in the big time.

THE BIG TIME

The sports world was hungry for a great heavyweight when Joe Louis arrived in New York in the spring of 1935.

It had been nine years since Gene Tunney took the title from Jack Dempsey in September of 1926 at Philadelphia's Sesquicentennial Stadium, where a record crowd of 120,000 fans paid $1.8 million to see the bout. It had been eight years since Tunney kept the title in their rematch, "the battle of the long count," getting off the floor before 105,000 fans who paid a record $2.1 million to see it.

There had not been a great heavyweight title bout since. Tunney retired with the title in 1928. The German, Max Schmeling, took the vacant title on a low-blow foul by Jack Sharkey in 1930, but lost it to Sharkey by decision in 1931. The Italian, Primo Carnera, took the title by knocking out Sharkey in 1933, but lost it by knockout to Max Baer in 1934. Shortly after he arrived in New York in 1935, Louis saw Baer lose the title to Jimmy Braddock.

None of those fighters was highly regarded. Baer was a powerful physical specimen with thunder in his fists, but he did not like boxing, did not train hard for his fights, and often clowned around in the ring. He knocked Carnera down 11 times in 11 rounds to win the championship, but took Braddock too lightly. He was out of condition and was outboxed by Braddock when he lost the crown.

Carnera was managed by Owney Madden and other mobsters, and there was talk that a lot of the fights that led to the title were fixed. We now know this to be true, but at that time it was only rumor.

Carnera, a former circus strong man in Italy, was six foot, six inches tall and weighed 260 pounds. He was of awesome size and tremendous strength. Although he looked clumsy, foe after foe had fallen before him. The beating Baer gave him was shocking and should have exposed his lack of boxing ability, but many still were not sure. They thought that maybe Baer had landed a lucky punch. Certainly, Carnera showed courage in getting up 10 times before going down for good.

Wanting to make more money yet out of their giant, Carnera's crew agreed to a bout with The Brown Bomber, the new sensation out of the Midwest. Mike Jacobs made the match for June 25 in Yankee Stadium. He thought it would draw a big crowd, make a lot of money, yet be an easy fight for Joe. Joe didn't know what to think. Poor Primo didn't know what to think. He never was told about the fixed fights. He thought he was too powerful for his foes. He wanted to think Baer really had just landed a lucky punch, but the beating had left him mixed up.

Louis was welcomed hungrily by the sportswriters. They met him at Grand Central Station when he arrived by train from Detroit and fired question after question at him. Joe didn't have the education, the vocabulary, the ability to speak he needed to deal with these sharpies, and he muttered answers. They described him as dumb, sullen, a hick "colored kid." But all felt he could fight and were excited by a bomber who might take the bad taste of the Carnera business out of their mouths.

Newspaper and newsreel photographers pushed one another aside to get pictures of this new fighter wherever he went. He was taken to City Hall to meet Mayor Fiorello LaGuardia. He was taken to Broadway to meet Jack Dempsey. Stories on him filled the sports pages of the newspapers and magazines. He had fought as a pro for less than a year, but he was fast becoming famous. Every fan in the east wanted to see The Brown Bomber in action.

Roxborough arranged for a room for Joe at an apartment owned by Lucille Armstead, a friend of Roxborough's wife. This was at 381 Edgecombe Avenue in The Bronx, a building where Duke Ellington, the great jazz musician, later lived a lot of his life. From his room, Joe could see Yankee Stadium.

To introduce him to the black community, he was booked into the Harlem Opera House at Seventh Avenue and 125th Street. He did an act with a black comic, Dusty Fletcher, who was so funny he could even make Joe's poker face break out in smiles.

Harlem was the most famous black community in the world and Joe was thrilled to be there. At the time, it was far from the vice-ridden ghetto it would become. There was a lot of night life there then.

Carnera's manager, Madden, owned the famous Cotton Club at Lenox Avenue and 140th Street. Louis met bandleaders Duke Ellington and Cab Calloway there and was introduced to Edna Mae Holly, who became Sugar Ray Robinson's first wife, and Lena Horne, the famous singer and a great beauty who became one of Joe's girl friends and lasted a long time with him.

At the famous Small's Paradise, where comedian Redd Foxx worked for many years, and where basketball star Wilt Chamberlain later became an owner, Louis met the great tapdancer Bill "Bojangles" Robinson, and was introduced to a gorgeous chorus girl, Marion Eggberg, who became another of his girl friends and visited him wherever he had fights for many years.

Joe was serious about Marva Trotter. She was the first girl he ever took home to meet his mother. His mother loved her and Joe loved her. He wanted to marry her. In a little while, he would. But, whether he had a wife or not, Joe also always had girl friends. Joe wound up having three wives. They all saw how he was with women, and left him mostly because of this.

But they all saw that this was his way and he wouldn't change. They saw that he treated them all well. Many of his wives and girl friends became friends and they'd meet and laugh about Joe's way with women as if he were a kid in a candy store.

Old Jack Blackburn didn't like the way Joe liked the ladies, but it was one argument he never won from Joe. Chappie didn't like Joe performing on stage and hanging out in night clubs in Harlem. He didn't like the characters Joe came into contact with. Before the Carnera fight, his manager, the mobster Madden, tried to muscle in on Louis's contract. "You're a nigger manager with a nigger fighter and you ain't goin' any place without us," one of the mob told Roxborough. He was offered $50,000 for half the contract. That was nothing compared to what they could make. Roxborough refused. He called friends in Detroit's "Purple Gang." They told him they did business with Madden's mob and would see to it that Madden backed off. He did.

On Blackburn's advice, Roxborough and Black went looking for a training camp far from The Big City. They found a place they could use at Pompton Lakes, New Jersey, an hour's drive from New York. It was a wooded area on a lake. There was a shaded area where they could pitch a ring and some stands for spectators. There was a barn they could convert to an indoor gym for use when the weather was bad. There were paths for running and bicycling. There was an old Colonial-style house where Joe and his managers could stay and a couple of cottages for the trainer and others who would work the camp.

The place was owned by Dr. Joseph Bier, a white dentist who was a fight fan. He vacationed there, but agreed to rent the place to the Louis group. Neighbors worried about the "niggers" who would be brought there. There were nasty newspaper articles, hate mail, and threatening telephone calls about this, but Doc Bier refused to back down. Louis not only stayed, but returned for most of his major fights. He drew large crowds here, white and black alike. The place became famous as Joe's place. Businesses in the area made a lot of money off Joe's place. Years later, the community gave a dinner for Joe to thank him for making them famous.

Joe loved the bright lights, but he was a country boy at heart and he loved that part of the country. He found the place peaceful and beautiful. It was restful for him, although he worked hard there. He was serious about his fighting as long as he fought and he almost always was willing to work hard to be fit to fight. He ran five or six miles early every morning and walked a few miles every evening. In between, he did calisthenics, shadow-boxed, hit the light and heavy bags, and sparred in the ring set up under the trees.

After a while, this drew large crowds who would pay two bucks a head to watch. They'd sit in the bleachers, which bordered the shaded ring on three sides. They'd come out on a Saturday or Sunday, mainly, and make a day of it. They'd sit there eating box lunches and talking boxing until Joe would come into the ring, wearing a white terrycloth robe and a white towel over his head. The talking would stop and there would be a hush. Manny Seamon, who became Blackburn's assistant, would take Joe's robe and towel and Joe would be wearing a white T-shirt and white woolen trunks and white tape on his hands.

He'd shadowbox and then they'd lace on his gloves and protective headgear, and a sparring partner such as George Nicholson would climb into the ring to work out with Joe. They fought regulation three-minute rounds and Louis worked hard and hit hard, and the fans thrilled to the fast hands and hard punches of The Brown Bomber. It would be so quiet you could hear the scraping of his shoes on the canvas as he shuffled forward. You could hear the wind rustling the leaves of the trees, and then you'd hear the grunting as he threw punches, and the thud of the big training gloves as they landed and small murmurs of excitement would rise in the crowd. In the end they'd give him a big hand, and he'd nod and wave as he went away.

There always were a lot of reporters there and they'd question Joe after training was done for the day. At first they were bothered that he didn't have much to say, but then they found out that he always meant what he did say. Later on, when there'd be a buildup to make a foe look better than he was, the promoters would plead with Joe to praise his opponent, but if Joe didn't think the fellow was much of a threat, he'd say so. He respected most of his foes. The writers didn't have to get in the ring to meet the foe—Joe did. He knew it was dangerous. He was meeting big, good fighters, who might not have been as good as he was, but were good enough to hurt him if they landed a good punch. But he never went along with the public relations game and never made his opponents out to be better than they were.

He didn't know about Carnera.

After the writers and fans had left, the place would be peaceful again. Joe always ate a big dinner and relaxed. He was always a big eater, but he worked hard and the food became muscle, not fat. After his morning run, Joe would eat a chunk of cheese and drink some fruit juice before he showered. Afterward, he had his breakfast—oatmeal, half a dozen eggs with ham steaks or sausage, thick slices of buttered bread, a lot of milk. He seldom had lunch, but he'd have an early dinner of thick steaks, salad, black-eyed peas, rolls, and milk. In the evening he'd put away a quart of ice cream. Bill Bottoms took care of him.

As the Carnera fight drew closer, the crowds grew larger. Extra security guards had to be hired to handle them. Concessions people sold hot dogs and soda pop, souvenir hats and pennants.

Two days before the fight, Joe was ready and returned

to his apartment in New York to rest. The morning of the fight, the fighters weighed in at the New York State Office Building and cops mounted on horseback had to clear the way for the foes. Carnera was measured in at just under six-foot-six and Louis at just under six-foot-three. Carnera was weighed in at 260½ pounds, Louis at 196. Carnera smiled crookedly and jabbered away in Italian, while Louis was silent and expressionless. Joe said, "He looked foolish to me."

People were growing suspicious of Primo's record until Ernie Schaaf died following a knockout at the hands of Carnera early in 1933. Later, it was revealed that Schaaf had suffered head injuries in a fight with Max Baer six months earlier, but at the time Schaaf died the giant Carnera looked dangerous. He took the title by knocking out Sharkey, although there were those who thought Sharkey just went down and stayed down. Carnera went home to Italy to defend the title, decisioning Spain's Paolino Uzcudun in 15 rounds in Rome. In Miami, he outpointed Tommy Loughran in 15. These were pretty good fighters. But Baer beat Carnera horribly in taking the title from him. Had Baer been the first who could not be bought off or scared off? Had Madden's mobsters thrown Carnera to the wolves?

After the Baer bout, Carnera won four straight, three by knockout, before he entered the ring against Louis. Carnera was seven years older at 28, he'd been fighting seven years longer, he was much the bigger. He'd been a national hero in Italy before the Baer bout, and Premier Benito Mussolini wired him that his nation was counting on him in the Louis fight.

Storm clouds were spreading over Europe. Hitler's Nazi Germany was building its military force to conquer Europe and impose white "Aryan supremacy." Mussolini's Italian Fascists were threatening black Ethiopia, which they would conquer. The loss to the Jew, Baer, had made Mussolini mad. He did not want Carnera now to lose to the black, Louis. Black groups visited Louis to tell him he represented blacks and Ethiopia in his fight with the Italian.

Louis was confused. He was not a political person. But he was a Negro, a "colored man" as he was called in those days, and he felt for his people. Later, he recalled, "Blacks put a lot of burdens on my shoulders. I was only twenty-one and I didn't know if I could carry that kind of weight. I didn't know how to handle acting for all my people. I just wanted to fight."

He did develop a friendship with one of the few black sportswriters, Billy Rowe, who became a sort of business partner to Joe. At Rowe's suggestion, Louis talked Jacobs into setting up another row of ringside seats for reporters representing black newspapers. Jacobs saw that it would be good business to attract the attention of those members of the black community who read the newspapers that specialized in news of blacks. It was the first time black writers had received press passes to a big fight.

Knowing that there were doubts about Carnera, Jacobs had scaled ticket prices low in the hope of drawing a big crowd. It paid off. More than 60,000 persons paid more than $300,000 to be there that night. The fans filled Yankee Stadium and Joe was awed by the attendance when, surrounded by protective police, he came out of his dressing room, up out of the dugout, and down the aisle to the ring. He later recalled, "That was the best night in all of my fighting. I couldn't believe that crowd. If you was ever a raggedy kid from the country and you come to something like that night, you'd know. I don't thrill to things like other people. I only feel good at certain things. I felt the best I ever felt that night."

In their corner, Blackburn told Louis to stay in close to Carnera so Primo could not use his reach advantage, to hit him in the body to bring his guard down, to go for the head when the big guy lowered his hands. The lights went out in the big ballpark, except for those over the ring. The great crowd hushed in nervous anticipation. Many of the fans were high up in the triple-tiered arena, far from the ring. The fighters seemed small from there.

There is nothing quite like a big fight in a big ballpark. A ball game is going to go nine innings or four quarters or whatever. A fight may end in ten seconds. The foes want to hurt each other. There are just the two of them in that little, spotlighted ring, fighting with their gloved fists and with great laurels and riches at stake. The fans start to holler when the bell rings.

Carnera at first tried to stay away and jab. Louis kept shuffling forward, moving in close, banging both fists to the body. Clumsily, Carnera tried to stay at a distance, jabbing, ready to throw his right hand. But he was slow and awkward and couldn't keep Louis away. If he'd gone right after him, Louis might have taken Carnera out right away, but he wasn't sure of himself and he was cautiously following Blackburn's instructions to concentrate on the body. He had difficulty getting through the guard of Carnera's large arms. One round passed, two, three, four.

Carnera pushed his punches and when he hit Louis he didn't hurt Joe. He tried to use his strength to wrestle Louis around, but Joe was in better shape and stronger. In the fifth round, Joe just lifted Carnera out of a clinch. Then he went to the head and hit Carnera with a right to the jaw and Primo looked dazed. Joe recalled, "I saw he had nothing. I knew I had him." Going into the sixth, Blackburn told Louis to "go get him." Louis got him.

Joe knocked him down with a right to the face. Primo got up with blood coming out of his mouth. Joe knocked him down with a right to the jaw. Primo struggled to his feet. Joe hit him with a left hook and right cross combination to the jaw and Primo went down for the third and last time. Referee Arthur Donovan, who was the leading referee in the ring at the time and would work many of Joe's bouts, waved his arms over the pitiful

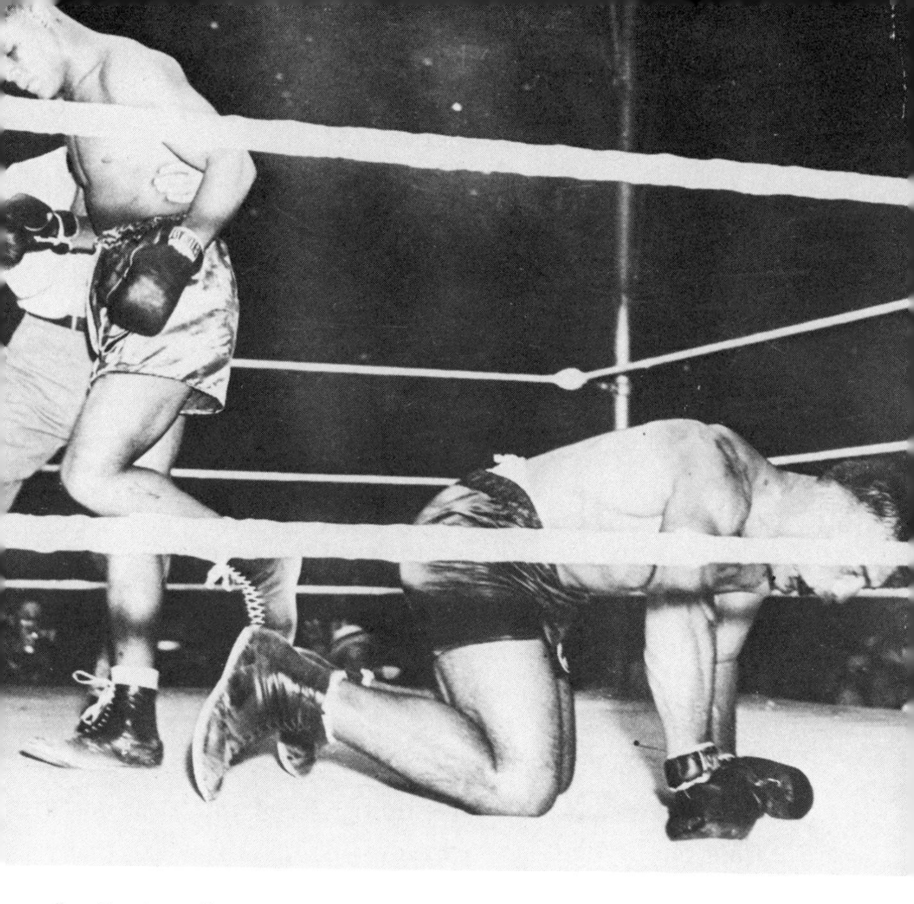

Joe Louis walks away from a bloodied ex-heavyweight champion, Primo Carnera, felled in the sixth round at Yankee Stadium, New York, June of 1935.

Italian, ending the bout. The crowd stood and cheered The Brown Bomber.

Louis had earned $60,000 in six rounds. He had been a professional fighter one week less than one year, and already he was filling a big ballpark with a phenomenal crowd and starting to make big money. Carnera had earned $60,000 also, but his managers took all of it, not half of it. His controversial career was coming to a close. He had made more than a million dollars, but he had none of it.

Carnera returned to the ring that winter and won a few fights. But no one would pay to see him any more and the mob abandoned him. In the spring of the following year, he was knocked out twice by little-known Leroy Haynes and suffered injuries that left his legs limp. He wound up in the charity ward of a hospital, far from home and alone.

It took him 18 months to recover enough to take a boat back to Italy. He tried to fight again. He lost his first comeback bout. Then he was knocked out in his next. And his next. He gave up the game and went home to his small village to farm for a living. He never really was sure what had happened to him.

Years later, he returned to the United States to live, refereeing boxing matches and wrestling for a living. Looked at as a freak, he was a fair attraction. He never said he knew he had been built up beyond his ability and he always said he was proud to have been a champion.

By that time, Joe Louis had become a boxing immortal.

FRIGHTENED FOES

After all but ending Carnera's career, Joe Louis went home to Chicago to spend some time with his fiancée, Marva Trotter. But Mike Jacobs wanted to cash in on Joe's sudden prominence. He booked The Brown Bomber into Comiskey Park, home of the White Sox, for an August 7th fight with Kingfish Levinsky, a ranking veteran and dangerous puncher. A crowd of more than 30,000 fans filled the ballpark, anxious to see Joe in action against a dangerous rival.

However, Joe's reputation preceded him. Although a veteran, Levinsky was awed by stories of Joe's punching power. He seemed so nervous in his dressing room before the fight, Jacobs was afraid he would duck out on the fight. He ordered that the bout begin a half-hour ahead of schedule. A member of the athletic commission asked why.

"Because it's gonna rain," Jacobs said.

The official looked at the sky, which was cloudless.

"Take my word for it, we better get it going," Jacobs said.

The official shrugged and ordered the fighters into the ring.

Before the fight, Levinsky would not look at Louis. At the bell, he seemed reluctant to leave his corner. When he did, he was stiff-legged and awkward. Louis hit him with a right hand to the head and his legs went soft. Levinsky swung a right, but Louis stepped inside it and hit him with a straight right to the head and Levinsky went down. He staggered up and Louis hit him with a left hook to the head and Levinsky went down on the ropes. He was sitting there while the referee counted ten over him. He was saying to the referee, "Don't let him hit me again. Please don't let him hit me again."

Louis was paid $53,000 for less than three minutes of work.

Big money beckoned him back to New York. A bout was set for six weeks later, September 24th, at Yankee Stadium against the ex-champ, Baer. There were those who thought Baer might be too much for Louis at the time. There were those who thought Baer could be one of the great fighters of all time, and that maybe the loss of his title to Braddock would now make him serious about boxing. Baer was a powerful fighter. His punches had killed Frankie Campbell early in his career and there were those who thought his punches had killed Ernie Schaaf, too, though Schaaf died after the Carnera fight.

Baer was only 26 and should have been at his best. He was much more experienced than Louis. He was as tall as Joe and heavier. He weighed 210, Joe less than 200. But Joe wasn't worried about Baer because he'd seen him lose to Braddock and hadn't been impressed. His widely quoted comment at the time was, "You can't tell me these are the two best heavyweights in boxing." He went into training at Pompton Lakes with a lot of confidence.

Louis was more worried about his love life. He was in love with Marva and wanted to marry her before she got away from him. She was starting to be suspicious of the life he led when he was away from her and the way he looked at other women. Joe's managers and trainers knew he went with other women. When he told them he wanted to marry Marva, they were happy because they thought he'd settle down.

However, they weren't happy when he wouldn't wait. They wanted him to wait until after the Baer bout. But he flew her in with her sister and her brother, a minister, and told them he wanted to marry her before the Baer bout. The night of the fight he woke up from his pre-fight nap at six, sneaked into an apartment with them, his managers and trainer and a few friends, and was married to her by her brother.

It was finished 15 minutes before he left for the Stadium at eight. It was unusual, to say the least, and those who knew what was going on worried that Louis would be distracted from his fight. But Joe wasn't bothered by much. He trained hard and took his fights in stride. He was sure he could take Baer easily.

So was Baer. Like Louis, Baer liked the ladies and the good life. Unlike Louis, Baer didn't like fighting or training. Unlike Louis, Baer clowned in and out of the ring. He later admitted that he was afraid of getting hurt in the ring and afraid of getting hurt by Louis and took the bout only for a big payday. Jacobs had said, "The fight'll make a million."

It did. Including press and other guests, there were more than 90,000 persons in the ballpark, including Mrs. Marva Louis in the 15th row, ringside. Some 88,150 paying customers paid $1,000,832 to see the fight. The million-dollar gate had been returned to the ring, and Joe would earn almost a quarter of a million dollars—$240,000—for another night's work.

Baer had Jack Dempsey working his corner—but he should have had Dempsey with him when he went out to fight. When Louis landed a left uppercut to Baer's jaw early in the first round, Baer blinked and said to himself, "I'm a dummy for doing this." He boxed away from Joe, who kept coming in the rest of the round. In the second, Joe caught Baer with blows that bloodied his nose and mouth.

At the bell ending the round, Joe dropped his hands and Baer landed a left and right to the jaw before the referee could get in between them. "That made me mad," Joe said later. In the third round he picked up the pace and punched powerfully. Near the end of the round, he landed a right to the jaw that floored Baer as the crowd started screaming. Baer arose at the count of nine, but a left hook dropped him again. The bell sounded at the count of four with Max down.

Between rounds, Dempsey tried to give his charge confidence. "He's hit you, but he hasn't taken you out. He can't hurt you," Jack said.

"Well, then, you better check the ref, because someone's beating the hell out of me out there," Baer muttered.

In the fourth, Louis landed a left hook and a right cross and Baer went down again. He was kneeling on one knee and shaking his head from side to side as if to say there was no point to this when referee Donovan counted ten over him and the fans stood and cheered The Brown Bomber. Later, Maxie admitted, "I was making a lot of money, but they couldn't pay me enough money to make me stand up and take more from that guy. They can't pay me enough to let a guy kill me. It was suicide to go on. I like life too much."

He went on enjoying the good life and making money for six more years in the ring. He beat some good fighters and lost to some good fighters, and knocked out a lot of bad fighters. He fought a lot of fighters who went on to fight Louis. Baer beat Tommy Farr and lost to Tommy Farr. Max knocked out Tony Galento in a bloody brawl and twice was knocked out by Lou Nova in bloody brawls. But he never asked for another round with Joe Louis.

Louis later said he never was better than against Baer. "I had hand speed that night like I never had any other night. I hit as hard as I ever hit. He didn't fight his fight, but after I beat him I felt for sure I could beat anybody." He had beaten two former champions and he wanted to make Jimmy Braddock a former champion, but Jacobs had trouble getting Jimmy to fight Joe.

Joe was getting a lot of fan mail, and his managers hired a secretary to handle his mail and appointments. They hired Russell Cowans, a black sportswriter and college graduate, who also was to tutor Joe two hours a day on grammar and other niceties. Cowans did put a little polish on Joe, and they became friends for the three years he stayed with Joe. He, more than anyone else, made Joe see how important he was to the black community. He was their hero, as if his success would make their life somehow better. They took pride in his performances and paraded through New York and Chicago and Detroit after his victories.

But Joe didn't want to be an idol; he wanted to enjoy his success. Invited by Bill "Bojangles" Robinson to watch him make a movie with child star Shirley Temple,

At 21, Joe Louis has just taken a wife, Marva Trotter, only a few hours before his knockout triumph over former champion Max Baer in New York in September of 1935.

Joe took Marva and his managers to Hollywood, where they partied with screen stars. Returning to Chicago, he moved Marva into a six-room apartment at 46th Street and South Michigan Avenue, where wealthy blacks were waited on. He showered furs and jewels on her. He bought new clothes for himself and a new car every year from then on.

All of Joe's friends bummed money from him. Meeting Jack Johnson, Joe was impressed that the ex-champ didn't ask him for any money. Jack was down and out. He picked up a few bucks working a "flea circus" on 42nd Street in New York or carnivals on the road. Although in his late fifties, he sometimes boxed exhibition bouts. Once in a while he was brought to meet a new champ and a publicist paid him a few bucks to pose with the titleholder.

Jack Blackburn hated Jack Johnson. Blackburn went out of his way to warn Joe not to lead the sort of life the last black heavyweight champ had, which would discredit him with the white fans. But Joe lived his own life. He did not parade his private life in public, however. And liberated white writers protected his image by not publicizing his lively life style. To the public, Joe was a shy, soft-spoken, simple "colored" lad who read daily from a large Bible his mama had sent him.

Jacobs brought Joe back to New York to fight Paolino Uzcudun in Joe's first fight in famed Madison Square Garden. John Reed Kilpatrick of the Garden wanted Joe in the Garden. With Joe, Jacobs was beginning to break Jimmy Johnston's grip on the Garden. The 20th Century Sporting Club was doing well. The bout was set for mid-December. Joe went back into training at Pompton Lakes, which he considered his good-luck camp by now.

Max Schmeling had beaten the Spaniard, Uzcudun, in 12 rounds in Berlin and wanted a chance to regain his title in a bout with Braddock. Jacobs wanted Louis to do better against Uzcudun than Schmeling had. Uzcudun was a big, strong guy, but he was another who was afraid of The Brown Bomber. Schmeling was at ringside the night of the fight, watching closely as Uzcudun came out in a low crouch, hands held high, both arms in front of his face to protect it.

Joe just jabbed and jabbed, hard, waiting for an opening. Uzcudun kept covering up, refusing to fight. The 18,000 fans who filled the Garden booed a bit and waited for Joe to land one of his bombs and earn the almost $40,000 he would receive for the fight. In the fourth round, Uzcudun spread his arms a few inches so he could see Joe. In that instant Joe's swift right hand flew. It tore between his foe's arms and landed on his mouth with such power it drove two of his teeth through his lower lip, and blood spurted out. A sickened Uzcudun staggered against the ropes and Joe hit him with a left and right that almost tore the Spaniard's head off. Uzcudun turned away, hanging on the ropes, refusing to fight back. Referee Donovan counted him out on his feet.

Uzcudun's American aide, Whitey Bimstein, who was to become one of the most famous fight trainers, later said, "I never saw any man hit another man as hard as Joe hit that Spaniard that night. It was scary. I don't blame him for being scared. Almost anybody would be."

But Schmeling said he wasn't. Interviewed by reporters and asked about his impressions of the new sensation, the German said, "I want to fight him for a chance at the title. I can beat him. I see something that tells me I can beat him." He wouldn't say what he saw, but he was a scientific fighter who felt he had spotted a flaw in Joe. No one believed him, but a buildup to a big fight had begun. It would be one of the biggest of Louis's life.

7

SCHMELING I

The future champion, Joe Louis, was matched with the former champion, Max Schmeling, in June of 1936 at Yankee Stadium. The winner was supposed to get a shot at the heavyweight title, held by Jimmy Braddock. Everyone assumed the winner would be Louis. Young and unbeaten, a murderous puncher, he was an 8–1 favorite.

Maximilian Adolph Otto Siegfried Schmeling was 31 years old. He had been a professional fighter for 13 years. It had been six years since he won the title on a foul from Jack Sharkey and four years since he lost it on a decision to Sharkey. The next year he had been knocked out by Max Baer. He had not fought for almost a year. Most figured he was finished.

But the German had lost only seven of 63 fights. He was smart and had a terrific right-hand punch. He had seen that Louis dropped his left hand when he went from the left jab to the left hook. He felt he could cross right-hand punches over Louis's lowered left. He was confident. He knew Louis was overconfident.

Louis said later, "I didn't give the German a second thought. He was washed up and never had been much. I was a big shot, the best in boxing, and everybody knew it, especially me. I didn't even want to train. I just wanted to have a good time."

To protect a big gate, Jacobs didn't want Louis to fight before the Schmeling match, but Joe's managers already had booked a bout with Charley Retzlaff in Chicago in mid-January. Joe and his wife went home for the holidays, then he flattened Retzlaff within one round.

Offered a movie role, film fan Joe jumped at the chance. He, his managers, and Marva returned to Hollywood. The picture was pointed at black audiences. Remotely resembling Louis's life, it was about a poor boy who becomes champion.

The Spirit of Youth was a bad picture. Joe was a bad actor, but he had a good time. The women chased the future champ and he didn't run very hard. He had an affair with Sonja Henie, the blond ice-skating queen from Norway, who was a movie star at the time. He gave Marva a mink coat to make up for it.

Marva's birthday also was in May. She turned 20 and Joe turned 22 in May. She went with him when he went to train at Lakewood, New Jersey, for his June bout. Joe's managers chose Lakewood because it had a big hotel, The Stanley, and could take care of more visitors than Pompton Lakes. It may have been a mistake.

After a while, Joe's manager thought Marva was distracting him and sent her home to New York. This may have been a mistake, too, as it left Joe on his own. But at that time he was going after golf more than girls. There was a big golf course in Lakewood, and Louis started a lifelong love affair with the game.

He'd cut short training routines to get to the golf course. He'd spend all day out there under a hot sun. He'd spend a lot of money losing bets to better golfers. Roxborough tried to run him off the course one time and Joe said he was a grown man and could do what he wanted to do. Joe later recalled, "I acted like a little boy."

He had not fought for more than five months when the Schmeling match arrived. Such a layoff is fine for mature fighters who have trained hard, but Joe was used to a fight a month his first two years as a pro, often two fights a month. He hadn't missed a month until he KO'd Carnera and missed only two months after he battered Baer.

Actually, the Schmeling fight completed 24 months as a professional fighter for Louis and he still had a lot to learn.

They went to New York to weigh in the morning of the scheduled bout, but it was raining and kept raining and the fight was postponed a day to the 19th. Louis weighed in four pounds heavier than Schmeling at 196 and spent the day and the next day waiting restlessly with Marva in his room at Harlem's Hotel Theresa.

Jacobs had expected 80,000 fans and a million-dollar

gate. Few thought Schmeling could compete with Louis, however. And some Jewish groups in heavily Jewish New York campaigned for fans to boycott the bout as a protest against the oppression of Jews in Nazi Germany. Then, another afternoon rain reduced walk-up sales, and only 40,000 turned out, paying a gross gate of only half a million.

Each fighter was in for 30 percent of the net receipts, and each received only a little more than $125,000.

Blackburn cautiously ordered Joe to jab until the older man tired. At the bell, he began to jab, jab, jab. The German with the slicked-down dark hair, thick dark eyebrows, and pale skin just kept retreating, his left hand high to protect his face, his right cocked. Tiring of caution, Louis went to a left hook late in the second round, but Schmeling drove his straight right over it and hit Joe in the mouth, surprising and hurting him.

Blackburn told Louis to go to the body in the third and Joe did. He couldn't get through the guard of the German to hit him in the head. But he had said he thought he could finish Schmeling within four rounds and in the fourth he went for the finisher.

A left hook cut Schmeling under the right eye. Louis went to throw another left hook. As Joe lowered his left from a jab to hook it, Schmeling drove over it with a straight right that landed squarely on Joe's jaw. Joe fell over backward and the fans came to their feet screaming.

All across the country, too, fans listening to the radio account of the contest were startled.

Knocked down for the first time as a professional, Joe was as startled as anyone. "I couldn't believe it," he later recalled. "I staggered right to my feet, but my eyes were blurred and my mind was blurred and I saw everything blurred from then on."

Joe was up at the count of four, but hurt terribly. He wobbled away across the ring as his foe moved in on him. Joe fell into a clinch as Max reached him. The knockdown had come with only 20 seconds left in the round, and the bell then saved Joe.

But, all later agreed, he lost the fight in that round.

Blackburn worked on Louis furiously before the fifth, pleading with him to keep his hands high. Joe tried, but every time he tried to fight back, Schmeling beat him to the punch. Every time Joe lowered his left after jabbing, Schmeling hit him with a straight right.

As the bell rang, ending the fifth, Louis dropped his hands and Schmeling hit him with a right that staggered Joe.

In the sixth, Schmeling hit Louis with so many rights that Louis was staggered several times, though somehow he stayed erect. The crowd was screaming for the kill. Joe's pal, Freddie Guinyard, led Joe's weeping, praying mother from the stands. Joe's stepbrother was yelling for Blackburn to stop the slaughter. Joe's wife had her head down, crying.

Blackburn was working on Louis between rounds, furiously trying to revive him, telling him he had to go to the body to tire out his foe. Dazed, Joe tried to do as he was told. From the seventh through the twelfth, Louis landed heavy blows with both hands to the body, but several landed low and referee Arthur Donovan awarded two rounds to the German on fouls.

Louis fought on, somehow, on instinct and courage. His knees buckled from a right-hand punch in the seventh and another in the ninth, but he battled on as his veteran opponent did seem to tire. Schmeling later admitted that his arms had begun to tire and he was waiting for a good opening to throw the punch that might finish off his foe. Louis hadn't landed a good punch to the head and Schmeling felt he could wait.

The crowd was in near hysteria as the bitter battle raged on.

Midway in the 12th round, Louis straightened up and went to left-hook Schmeling. Max sent his right straight over Joe's lowered left and it landed flush on the left side of Louis's jaw. Joe reeled backward. Max went after him and landed another right that sent Joe back into the ropes. Joe wobbled off the ropes as though drunk, and Max hit him with a right hand, another, and another.

Another right and Louis's legs gave way; he fell to the floor on his back. He rolled over on his stomach and tried to push himself erect as the referee picked up the count from the timekeeper. As ten was tolled over him, he fell flat on his face. Louis later said, "I heard the counting as if it came from far away, but I was sleepy and it didn't mean nothing to me. If I tried to get up,

An exultant Max Schmeling stands in the background as Arthur Donovan, the referee, completes the ten count over a fallen Joe Louis in Yankee Stadium upset, June, 1936.

it was instinct. I didn't know what was happening. I just wanted to lay there and sleep."

Standing in a neutral corner, Schmeling grinned broadly. The fans were standing on their feet hollering their surprise. Blacks in the stadium and across the country bent their heads, and some wept with disappointment. Their hero had fallen and presumably was finished. Joe had to be helped to his corner, and it took ice water and smelling salts to bring him around enough to make any sense of what had happened to him. They helped him to his dressing room and closed it to the press.

In his room, a joyous Schmeling announced, "I will be the first former champion ever to recapture the heavyweight title. I will beat Braddock as I beat Louis."

In the next day's Chicago *Tribune*, Wilfred Smith wrote, "Max Schmeling ended Joe Louis's reign of terror tonight. . . .

"In one of the greatest surprises in the history of the prize ring, the former heavyweight champion of the world knocked out the Brown Bomber in the twelfth round. . . .

"Schmeling, the man the world pitied, who everybody said was doomed to certain defeat, dominated the battle. His terrific right-hand punches, delivered unerringly with pile-driver power to Louis's jaw, sent the Bomber to the floor. . . .

"A crowd of 39,878 watched the uneven bout. They came to see another quick, stirring triumph for the colored lad who had beaten two former world champions and struck fear to the hearts of a score of opponents.

"They remained to see Schmeling hammer Louis to unconsciousness. . . . Schmeling, who held the coveted heavyweight title for two years, also earned the right to meet the present champion, Jimmy Braddock, for that title.

"Louis now must begin again a long, tedious climb to the championship which he thought was his for the asking. It remains to be seen whether he will ever scale the height. But tonight the question, 'Can Louis take it?' was answered. Louis showed that he could absorb punishment for a much longer time than many thought he could."

In the next day's New York *Times*, James P. Dawson wrote, "In one of the greatest heavyweight battles of modern ring history, Max Schmeling, sturdy, solid German, who formerly held the world heavyweight title, last night provided one of the ring's biggest upsets when he knocked out Joe Louis, Detroit's famed Brown Bomber. . . .

"Exactly 2 minutes, 29 seconds of the fatal 12th had gone into history when Louis, hailed as the king of fighters entering the ring, was counted out. . . .

"The crowd witnessed a form reversal that was greater even than that in which James J. Braddock lifted the heavyweight title from Max Baer last year. And it was Schmeling, with the might of his right fist his chief weapon of attack, who hammered his way into another chance at the title he lost to Jack Sharkey.

"Schmeling was the underdog in betting odds of 8 to 1 as the fight started. Bettors were offering even money he wouldn't come up for the fifth round. . . .

"But Schmeling, ignoring the contempt in which he was held as a foe for the Bomber, with the latter's unbroken string of 27 victories that held 23 knockouts, fulfilled the promise he made that he would fight his way into another crack at the title.

"The German is now undisputed challenger for Braddock's crown. None who saw last night's upset would contradict Schmeling's bold assertion that he will be the first man in all ring history ever to regain the heavyweight championship."

But, like life, sports take funny turns at times. Seeing Schmeling batter Louis, Braddock was not sure he wanted to take on the veteran's right-hand haymakers for the title. Suddenly, Louis seemed easier than Schmeling. And promoter Mike Jacobs was not about to give up on Louis and let Schmeling have whatever he wanted.

It figured that Louis was finished as a championship contender. Only a few fighters ever recovered from a beating like that one, especially early in their careers. Joe's confidence should have been shattered. But it turned out that he had determination and the strength of character to carry on.

On the long, lonely train ride back to Chicago, Chappie told Joe, "Everything happens for the best. This'll make you a better fighter. It'll learn you that you can't take a thing lightly when you walk into the ring. He took advantage of a mistake you made. Well, you're young and you make mistakes. All you got to do is learn from your mistakes and not make them again.

"You're better than him and you'll be ready for him and you'll beat him when you get him again."

Years later, lying in bed in Los Angeles, remembering

the good days and the bad days, Joe said, "That was the worst day of my life. I hadn't figured out what had gone wrong. I felt foolish, embarrassed. I figured Blackburn just tryin' to buck me up.

"But, after Blackburn showed me what I'd done wrong, I felt better because I figured I didn't have to do it no more. I figured I'd blown my title chance, but I wasn't thinkin' about titles right then, all I was thinking about was that German who'd beaten me so bad, and how bad I wanted to beat him back.

"You forget bad things fast and it took me a few weeks but soon I was thinking good again, how maybe I could come back and overcome this thing. I didn't like people figuring I was finished. I was twenty-two years old—how could I be finished? I could still fight. I figured I could fight my way back, somehow, if I got the chance."

TAKING THE TITLE

One of the bad things about boxing is that the best fighters don't have to fight one another for chances at championships and champions don't have to defend their titles against the most deserving challengers. In sports with schedules, such as baseball, a team has to meet all foes the year after taking a title, but in boxing promoters and managers maneuver for matches.

Following Schmeling's knockout of Louis, Max clearly was the most deserving contender for the heavyweight title. Braddock, the champion, was under exclusive contract to Madison Square Garden. Jimmy Johnston signed Schmeling to meet Braddock for the title at Madison Square Garden Bowl on Long Island on June 3, 1937. Reluctantly, Braddock agreed.

Meanwhile, unable to get Schmeling to agree to a rematch with Louis, Mike Jacobs, who held the exclusive contract to promote Joe's bouts, negotiated with Joe Gould, who was Braddock's manager, for the champion to defend his title, instead, at Comiskey Park, Chicago, on June 22.

Mike Jacobs, Joe's promoter, offers advice to Louis in July, 1936, following The Brown Bomber's first defeat.

Jacobs and Gould were Jewish and sought sympathy from the public for their not wanting Schmeling to take a title back to Nazi Germany. Privately, Jacobs gave Gould a contract calling for Gould and Braddock to get ten percent of the net receipts from Mike's heavyweight title promotions, if any, for ten years. (There would be many, but Gould would have to sue to get his share.)

Meanwhile, Mike set out to build back The Brown Bomber to public favor. Louis wanted to lay off a little while, but Jacobs wanted to bring him right back into the spotlight. Louis was home while his sick stepfather, Pat Brooks, died, but then Joe returned to Pompton Lakes, "his lucky camp," to resume training. Convinced now that hard work was necessary to make full use of his skills in this risky business, he went back to the sort of dedicated training he had done before. He was booked back into Yankee Stadium to meet ex-champ Jack Sharkey in mid-August, only two months after the Schmeling loss.

Sharkey had defeated Schmeling for the title four years earlier, had defeated such formidable foes as Harry Wills, Mike McTigue, and Young Stribling, had fought to a draw with the great Mickey Walker, and had given a good account of himself before being knocked out by Jack Dempsey earlier in his career. His image was soiled when he lost his title to Primo Carnera, but he was still a big name. However, he had won only two of his last seven fights, and at 33 he was through. He hoped his right hand could do to Louis what Schmeling's had, but Jack was not the puncher Max was.

Blackburn had drilled Louis on keeping his left high, looking for right leads, blocking them, and counter-punching. Joe went into his comeback bout looking for rights and that's about all he saw. One landed in the opening round, but Joe shook it off. He blocked one in the second round, threw his own, landed, and knocked down his foe. He countered rights with rights in the third round and knocked down his foe three times. The third time, Sharkey stayed down. As an attraction, it was a bust—fewer than 15,000 fans turned out, and Joe earned only about $35,000. But he was back in business.

Three weeks later, Louis was in Philadelphia to face local favorite Al Ettore at Sesquicentennial Stadium, scene of the first Tunney-Dempsey fight. Before the bout Ettore sat in his corner calmly talking to and laughing with friends at ringside, as if he had nothing to fear. Within five rounds he lay on a lower rope, blood dripping from his face. The fight pulled in more than 25,000 fans and Louis earned more than $50,000. Less than three weeks later, Louis picked up $8,000 putting out an Argentine, Jorge Brescia, in three rounds at the old Hippodrome in New York.

It was commonplace for top fighters of the time to box a lot of exhibition bouts, strutting their stuff for fans who might not otherwise get to see them. This was long before television, mind you. It was an easy way for top fighters to pick up a thousand dollars or so here and there. Usually they took it easy. But The Brown Bomber bombed away in these bouts and, even with both fighters wearing big gloves and headgear, scored a lot of knockouts, especially early in his career. Before and after the Christmas holidays in 1936, Joe scored five consecutive KOs in exhibition bouts—two on one night in New Orleans, two on another in South Bend, Indiana.

In mid-December, Louis took on Eddie Simms in a 10-rounder in Cleveland for $20,000. He took him out in 26 seconds of the first round for his fastest-ever knockout. A left hook flattened Simms for the ten-count. Afterward, he spoke nonsense when the referee tried to talk to him. "Let's go up on the roof. I want to get some fresh air," Simms said.

Early in January, 1937, Joe KO'd Steve Ketchell in two rounds in Buffalo. Late in January Joe was booked back into Madison Square Garden with Bob Pastor. Joe got the booking because Bob was Jimmy Johnston's fighter. Jimmy wanted Joe to look bad. An N.Y.U. graduate, Pastor was a smart fighter, but Johnston had him running the entire ten rounds. Joe won the decision and earned $36,000, but he looked bad.

Jacobs brought Joe back three weeks later in Kansas City with Natie Brown. Brown had made Louis look bad in his big fight in Detroit almost two years earlier when Jacobs brought in the New York press to see Joe in action. Brown had defended, backpedaled, clinched, and lasted ten rounds. But he wasn't as fast on his feet as Pastor. And Joe was a better boxer, now. Louis KO'd Brown in four rounds and picked up a fast $11,000.

At this point, Jacobs and Joe Gould got together and agreed to terms for the June 22 title bout in Chicago between Braddock and Louis. Braddock was given 50 percent of the net gate and radio and movie money. He was guaranteed at least $500,000. Gould and Braddock were given 10 percent of Jacobs's heavyweight title promotions for ten years whether or not Louis took the title. Joe was given 17½ percent of the net gate with no guarantees. But he also was the first black man in almost thirty years to be given a shot at the heavyweight title.

John Reed Kilpatrick took Jacobs and Gould to court, claiming the Garden had exclusive rights to Braddock's fights, but a judge ruled that since Braddock was guaranteed nothing in return for those rights, the contract was invalid.

Kilpatrick and Johnston continued to claim it had an agreement with Gould for Braddock to defend his title June 3rd in Madison Square Garden Bowl. It sold tickets for such a fight. Schmeling came to this country and went into training in upstate New York for such a fight. Braddock was in training, too, but for another fight entirely. The Schmeling–Braddock bout became known as "the phantom fight." Right up to the day of the fight, Johnston insisted that Braddock had to show up. But that night the Bowl was empty and dark and there was no fight. Ticket money had to be refunded to the purchasers.

Meanwhile, Louis and Braddock continued to train for their forthcoming fight in Comiskey Park, a real fight for a real title. In the four months between Louis's last bout and the big Braddock bout, Jacobs did not want Joe to take any chances. First, he hired a private railroad car and sent him on a western tour of exhibition matches. Then he rented a $100,000 mansion for Joe and his group in Milwaukee, Wisconsin, and set up a training camp in nearby Kenosha, on the shores of Lake Michigan. Joe arrived at camp about the time of his twenty-third birthday and trained hard for six weeks. It was unusual for a challenger to be the favorite, but Louis was a 2–1 favorite going into the fight.

James Joseph Braddock, out of New York City, had been labeled "Lucky Jim." A lot of bad luck in his life had changed into good luck when he took the title. Turning pro in 1926, he went 38 fights without losing before he was beaten. He flattened most of his foes with a strong right-hand punch. Then things started to go bad.

He broke his right hand three times. He broke two ribs. He broke his collarbone. From 1929 through 1933, he won 14 fights and lost 16. These were the Depression days and he wasn't training for fights because he had to work for a living—when he could get work. He did dirty work, lifting heavy loads on the shipping docks and in the railroad yards. He was out of work and on relief a lot. He made less than a hundred dollars for some fights.

He had a wife and three children and had to borrow money to feed his family. His life was sad and his once promising ring career seemed all but over. But Joe Gould wouldn't give up on him. Jimmy Johnston needed an opponent for Corn Griffin, a promising prospect he wanted to show off on the Carnera–Baer title card in

1934. Gould talked Johnston into taking Braddock because the faded fighter posed little threat to Griffin.

Griffin knocked down Braddock in the first round of their fight. But Braddock was so hungry and desperate that he would not give up on what was his last chance. He got up and fought back, and got to Griffin in the third round with a right hand that cooled off the hot prospect. Jim made $250 and was happy to get it.

In November of 1934 he got another fight, with John Henry Lewis, a black fighter out of Los Angeles who looked as if he was on his way to the light-heavyweight title. He did, in fact, take the title from Bob Olin the following year, with the young Joe Louis on the scene in St. Louis, blazing a bit of a trail for Louis. But late in 1934 Braddock decisioned him to climb another step back up the ladder and pick up a badly needed $700.

In March of 1935 Braddock was matched with Art Lasky, who was being built up for a title fight with Max Baer. Braddock beat him, earned his first fair pay night, $4,100, and suddenly it was Braddock in there with Baer in Max's first title defense.

Braddock was a 10–1 underdog and Baer did not take him seriously. Braddock won, as an out-of-shape Baer clowned away his crown. Braddock made $50,000 and suddenly he was "The Cinderella Man."

He had not fought for two years and the Louis fight was Braddock's first defense of his championship. He was 31 years old and no one knew what he had left. But he had battled back from oblivion and no one now could take him lightly.

A turnout of 45,500 fans filled Comiskey Park on the night of June 22, 1937. Among them were former heavyweight champions Jack Dempsey and Gene Tunney, light-heavyweight champion John Henry Lewis, and welterweight champion Barney Ross, who were introduced in the ring. Braddock, an Irishman, wore a green robe with a white shamrock on it. Louis wore a blue robe, trimmed in red. Braddock wore white trunks, Louis purple trunks. In his corner waiting for the first bell, Louis was told by Blackburn, "Chappie, you gonna be champ tonight."

The outer lights went out in the old ballpark, the bell rang, and the two moved out to meet under the overhead spotlights. The big crowd drew in breath. Braddock came out punching. It was surprising. He had been expected to be cautious, defensive, wary of The Brown Bomber's bombs, but he wanted to catch Louis by surprise and he was looking to land right-hand punches as Schmeling had. Surprised, defensive, Louis jabbed and moved back, which was not like him.

Louis landed a right to the side of Braddock's head, but the champion countered with a short right uppercut to Joe's jaw. It was a hard punch and it landed flush. Louis's legs went out from under him and he landed on the canvas. Later, he said, "It took me off my feet, but it didn't hurt me all that much. I was surprised by it and I didn't know what to think, but I could think. I wasn't jarred out of my senses like in the Schmeling fight, and I jumped right to my feet."

As Louis got up, Braddock went to get him, throwing right-hand haymakers, but Louis blocked most of them and threw a left hook and right cross that hurt Braddock at the bell.

The fans were standing and shouting at the wild action. The radio announcer was shouting into his microphone. Across the country, fans were shouting. It looked as if Louis couldn't take a punch. It looked as if Braddock was about to score yet another upset.

In the ballpark and across the country, black fans were worried. The Brown Bomber was their hero, and they hoped the Schmeling loss had been an accident. Asked if he had let his people down, Louis had said, "I lost, they didn't. Me winning don't make them no richer. Me losing don't make them no poorer." Yet, they counted on him and it looked as if he was letting them down again.

Braddock went to finish off Louis in the second round. He threw right hand after right hand. Hollered at by Blackburn for not taking a count of nine to regain his composure, warned to box carefully for a while, Louis blocked the punches and boxed. Braddock grew wild and Louis stepped inside to shake the champ with left hooks and straight rights.

Seeing that he did not have the challenger hurt, Braddock began to back off and box him, looking for another right-hand opening. In the third, Louis caught Braddock with a left that tore open his left lip. By the fourth, Braddock was bleeding quite a bit. In the fifth, a left by Louis tore open another cut on the left side of his foe's forehead.

Braddock was slowing down and Louis was picking up the pace. In the sixth, Louis started to land heavily on his bleeding and bruised rival. Braddock battled back gamely. It meant a lot to him to be champion, he'd been through a lot, and he was not about to give up. But near the end of the seventh, Braddock began to pull away from Joe's rights. Louis landed a left hook that staggered Jimmy, but the bell saved him.

By the eighth, he had little left. He was worn out and wide open. He tried a right hand at the bell, but Louis blocked it and hit him with a right. Joe jolted Jimmy with a left to the jaw, then hurt him with another left to the body. Louis hooked his left to the head, opening another cut over Braddock's left eye. Desperate, Braddock threw a wild right that missed. Louis stepped inside it and drove a right hand hard to Braddock's face. It was a brutal blow, landing right on the champion's chin. He fell forward on his face.

The fans were roaring as the challenger walked to a neutral corner and referee Tommy Thomas started to count over the champion. At five, the stunned "Cinderella Man" struggled to a sitting position, but he could not get up. At ten, he was an ex-champ and the challenger was champion. At one minute and 20 seconds of the eighth round that night in 1937, The Brown Bomber was the new champion of the world, the first black heavy-

The Brown Bomber takes the heavyweight title as James J. Braddock hits the deck in the eighth and last round at Comiskey Park, Chicago, June of 1937. Referee Tommy Thomas is ready to count out the loser.

weight titleholder since 1915 and, at 23, the youngest champion in history.

"The winner and new heavyweight champion—Joe Louis!" the announcer roared, and the fans that June night in Chicago cheered. In Chicago and Detroit and New York and cities across the country, black men and women and children who had sat tensely by their radios and listened to the blow-by-blow account of the bout and cheered the end went out in the streets to celebrate, and improvised parades of victory.

It meant a lot to them. There was black baseball, but there were no blacks in big-league baseball. There were no blacks in big-league football. Blacks weren't even allowed by law to box whites in many states, although the law had been changed in some places Louis had fought. Now a "colored man" was heavyweight champion, the most coveted title in sports, and Negroes across the country took tremendous pride in it, as though in the doing of it he had done much for them.

Most whites did not know what to think. Most were not bigoted, but seventy years had passed since the slaves had been freed following the Civil War, and blacks were just beginning to gain their rights. They still were segregated in the South, and still struggled for equality elsewhere. Whites had to get used to this. They liked Louis—he seemed a likable lad, and a terrific fighter. It was hard not to admire such a terrific fighter.

But what about Schmeling? Hadn't the German beaten Louis? Didn't he deserve the title fight more than the Detroit lad? With 35 victories, 30 by knockout, The Brown Bomber had shot to the top in just three years of fighting as a professional, and at the age of 23 years and one month was just approaching his peak. But there was that one loss, by knockout, to mar his record.

In his quarters that night, in his half of the White Sox

dressing room, separated from his foe by a wooden partition, Joe Louis was asked how it felt to be champ, and he said, "Don't nobody call me champ till I beat that Schmeling." It had been a hard night and that still hung heavy on his head. Joe was sore, weary, unsmiling, as poker-faced as ever.

It was worse on the other side of the room, where a bloodied and bruised Braddock wept. "I thought I had him at first. I gave my best. I was pretty good, wasn't I?" Braddock asked. The newsmen with him agreed he'd given a good account of himself.

Years later Braddock said, "If I'd hit him a good one after I knocked him down I'd have had him, but I didn't. Joe was always in trouble with punches to his head, but he was always getting out of trouble. He was smart enough to keep covered up.

"He hit me with more punches that night than I got hit in my other eighty-seven fights. I never got hit much. I never got cut much. But he cut me twenty-three stitches' worth. The right hand to my mouth that flattened me drove a tooth right through my mouthpiece and lip.

"What power that guy had! When he knocked me down I could have stayed there for three weeks. But I'm glad I got to fight him because I made a good fight with him and he was one of the greatest fighters in history, maybe the greatest.

"That was some night," Braddock concluded.

All that night, blacks marched through the streets of

the big cities, honking horns, burning bonfires, and cheering their champion. In Chicago they stood outside the new champion's house on South Michigan Avenue and cheered until he and his wife came out and waved to them and smiled on them.

Inside, family and friends had gathered to greet the new king, but he took time to telephone his thrilled mother back in Detroit and she told him there were hundreds outside her home, hollering happily at her.

"It was some kind of night," Joe Louis recalled later. "A man don't have many nights like that."

Most men never have any.

A FIGHTING CHAMPION

In the Chicago *Tribune*, Arch Ward's story read: "Dour-faced Joe Louis, only three years out of Chicago's Golden Gloves, is the heavyweight champion of the world. He won the title by knocking out Jimmy Braddock in the eighth round at Comiskey Park last night in the most thrilling match the ring had produced since the battle of the famous long count at Soldiers Field ten years ago.

"The fight was a classic. Financially it was not the success promoters had hoped. The paid attendance was said to be less than 50,000 and the receipts were less than $600,000.

"Braddock came up to the last round worried, cut, bleeding, and a forced smile on his lips. He had survived 21 minutes which threatened time after time to turn into disaster. He was defending the championship against bitter odds, but he was defending it.

"Suddenly, from out of the sparring that began the eighth round, Louis shot a terrific right . . . The blow travelled only a foot . . . Braddock sank on his side

. . . It was at least two minutes before Braddock regained his senses.

"Through all this, the fleeting actions of a few seconds, a low rumble had started, the distant thunder of the gallery gods heralding a storm. It came from the bleachers far out in center field where many of the Louis adherents were watching. It came from the right field and left field stands, outstripping any electrical eruption for speed, swelling into a mad roar as tier after tier of spectators caught it up . . . It was bedlam, nothing less . . ."

When they completed the count, the crowd of 45,500 had paid gross receipts of $715,470, which left a net of about $600,000 after promotional expenses were removed. Braddock got his guaranteed $500,000, including money from movies, which were shown in theaters across the country starting the next day. After Louis was paid his percentage, which came to $103,684, Jacobs was left with a loss. But Louis had the title and Jacobs had Louis.

One of the reasons the gate was less than it might have been was that while top tickets to heavyweight title fights at the time sold for $25 to $50 depending on the match, Joe asked Jacobs always to set aside some seats at $5 to $10 or less for the poor people. Bleacher seats for the Braddock fight went for only $3.50, and this enabled a lot of poor blacks from the surrounding South Side ghetto to go to the fight.

It was these fans that thundered their approval of the

new champ in such a stirring way. All was madness that night in that old ballpark when The Brown Bomber reached the heights.

Years later Louis said, "I knew I was going to make me a lot of money, but it wasn't the money that mattered to me. All money meant to me was spending it, and I sure knew how to do that. The title was what mattered. What the title meant to me was Max Schmeling had to fight me again. Braddock didn't want to fight me again, but Max did. Max didn't think no colored boy could beat him. Max was a fool.

"Maybe my people were pulling for me, but I never thought nothing about being black and I never felt no pressure. I just thought about being a boxer and being the best and being champion. I just didn't feel like I was really champion until I beat that Schmeling. But I remember the day I took the title like it was yesterday.

"It was hot that day. I drove down from Wisconsin with my people and went to an apartment. Jack Blackburn stayed with me. The middle of the afternoon we went for a walk for about an hour. Then I went to bed and slept soundly until they woke me and told me it was time to go to the stadium. The heat didn't bother me. The fight didn't bother me. Those days, nothing bothered me. I just went to bed and went to sleep.

"I remember coming out of the dressing room and thinking it was a pretty good crowd, but it's a small ballpark and the crowd looked bigger than it was. I remember being knocked down and thinking I was about to make a fool of myself and I was going to blow my big chance. But I'd always thought about how good it would be to get knocked down and get up and go on to knock the other man out.

"I remember Braddock's manager yelling all through the seventh round for Braddock to keep up his left. It's still so fresh in my mind: 'Keep your left up, keep your left up, keep your left up.' I said to myself between rounds the first time Braddock moves his left up when Gould yells, I'm going to move in and hit him. I was just waiting for it.

"When he raised the left, I hit him with a left hook to the belly and crossed a right to the chin. You could have counted over him all night. I was never nervous until they held my hand up. Then it came to me I was champion. It was scary. I'll never forget it. My legs shook when they led me back to the dressing room. When I got there, I felt faint. I lay down on the dressing room table.

"After a few minutes, I was all right. I sat up and they let the reporters in. They got in one another's way getting in that door. They were anxious to get at me. There were so many of them. They wanted to know what it felt like to be champ. I told them not to call me champ till I beat that Schmeling. But I knew I was champ and it felt good. I guess few guys ever get that feeling all their lives. I thought to myself I wanted to do good by that title.

"I thought to myself I was never going to give it up.

But I was young then and I didn't know what it was to get old."

The young champion took some time off. A baseball fan who rooted for the Detroit Tigers, he had formed The Brown Bomber Softball Team, a group of black athletes from his home town who toured the country in a fancy bus with Joe footing the bills. Joe joined them from time to time, from town to town, as an extra added attraction. He played first base and took at least one turn at bat before retiring to the coaching lines. He was a powerful right-hand hitter, naturally. And when he played, he pulled in good crowds and the team made money. After the Braddock bout, he toured with the team for a spell, while his managers and promoters worried he'd get hurt.

Dropping off the tour, he visited every available golf course, playing one or two rounds a day, getting to be pretty good at the game, but not good enough not to blow a lot of dough gambling on it. He played with a lot of prominent personalities at a lot of private clubs where blacks previously had not been permitted to play. Loving horses, he bought horses and a $100,000 spread of 440 acres, Spring Hill Farm, in Michigan where he and Marva learned to do show riding and jumping, won some ribbons, and brought blacks into the all-white world of horse shows.

With his popularity, he began to break down a lot of barriers for blacks, although he was welcomed many places that still barred other blacks. He ate in a lot of restaurants and attended a lot of night clubs that had barred blacks, and some did lower the barriers after that. He liked the night life and the big bands. Duke Ellington and Jimmy Lunceford were his favorites, and he played their records on a player he took with him wherever he went on the road. He bought fancy clothes and fancy cars and went fancy places. He bought expensive gifts for his girl friends.

He also bought expensive gifts for his wife, his mother, his sisters, including cars and fur coats. He was generous to a fault with his family. He bought his mother a house and a farm and took care of all her needs. He helped his sisters and brothers buy houses. He staked his sister Emmarell to a hat shop in Detroit and she made a success of it. He sent his sister Vunice through college and later said, "The day she graduated when I walked across the Howard University campus with our mama was the proudest day of my life." He bought her a brand-new Buick as a graduation present.

He also put a sister with a drinking problem into a private hospital and paid all her bills while she recuperated. And when his father was found to be still alive and still in the mental institution back in Alabama, Joe paid all his bills from then to the day his dad died in 1938. Authorities in Alabama contacted the champion a day or two after he took the title. From that day, Joe was expected to pay his way. And pay and pay and pay. For everyone.

Joe had to fight. He had to make money. He spent it

fast. Jacobs wanted him to fight so they could make money. Roxborough and Black wanted him to be a fighting champion. They thought that because of his color he had to be better than other champions. Joe didn't mind. He liked fighting. He went to the big fights wherever they were held across the country. And he wanted to be a fighting champion. He wanted to fight Schmeling first, but Jacobs wanted to wait to build that one up.

Looking for a colorful foe for the new champ, Jacobs came up with Tommy Farr, heavyweight champion of Great Britain. The former coal miner from Wales was a rugged guy. He was almost as tall as Joe and heavier. He fought at about 205 pounds, while Joe was fighting at 197 at that time. Farr was Joe's age, 23. He'd decisioned Max Baer in 12 rounds in London in April. He was a worthy challenger. He had agreed to fight Schmeling for the right to challenge Joe, but when the Jacobs offer came along, poor Max was shut out again.

The match was made for Yankee Stadium on August 26, less than nine weeks after Louis took the title Braddock had held without defending it for two years. Louis was rushed back into training camp at Pompton Lakes and he punished sparring partners at $25 a day. Baseball's Babe Ruth and Joe DiMaggio, track star Jesse Owens, tap dancer Bill Robinson, and even Max Schmeling visited camp to watch Joe train.

On fight day, Joe went to New York to weigh in. It was raining. It rained all day. The fight had to be postponed. Ticket sales weren't as good as expected, anyway.

No one knew Farr. He'd never fought in this country. It continued to rain and Jacobs continued to postpone the fight. Joe went back to camp. But he'd lost his edge. He'd built up to a peak and now he suffered a letdown.

By Monday, the 30th, he just wanted to get it over with. The fighters returned to New York. Farr weighed in at 204½ pounds, Louis at 197, a quarter-pound lighter than he'd been for Braddock. There were 32,000 people in the ballpark that night and they paid $325,000 to see the fight. Louis earned a little over $100,000 and Farr picked up a guaranteed $60,000. They earned their money.

Farr proved durable. He fought with his fists in front of his face and he bobbed and weaved in an awkward style that puzzled Joe. Farr threw a lot of punches and punched with a lot of strength. Joe claimed later that he hurt his right hand hitting Farr high on the head in the third round and didn't hit hard with the hand after that or he would have knocked him out within five rounds.

He did hit Tommy with a left hook in the fifth that hurt Tommy, and Joe felt it was the hardest punch he landed all night, but Tommy took it. Louis landed two more left hooks to the head and two to the body that wobbled the Welshman, but Farr held on and lasted to the bell. Louis hurt him with left hooks in the seventh, but Farr held on and lasted to the bell. In the second half of the fight, Farr fought back bravely. It was as though he felt he'd taken Joe's best shots without caving in and it gave him a lift.

The press and public were astonished as the bout went on without Farr's falling and with the Welshman fighting back and even bruising one of Joe's eyes. Blackburn felt Joe was ahead on points and didn't want him to risk getting his eye cut open and maybe having the match stopped, so he pleaded with Joe to play it safe. Joe's jab was piling up points, but he couldn't penetrate Tommy's defense too well, anyway. Joe shook up Tommy near the end of the 13th, but he couldn't put him down.

When the bell rang ending the 15th round, there was surprise ringside and radioside, but the two judges and referee made the champion a unanimous winner. One judge, McPartland, voted for Louis 9 rounds to 6; the other, Lynch, favored Louis 8 rounds to 6 with 1 even, while referee Donovan had Joe a one-sided winner by 13 rounds to 1 with 1 even.

In his dressing room, the bruised Briton sighed and said, "I gave my bloody best." In his room, a bruised Bomber said, "I wasn't at my best." He had badly bruised knuckles on his right hand, which were encased in a cast while they healed. Later, Louis said, "Farr was the toughest fighter I ever fought. He took a punch better than any man I ever hit."

However, it hadn't been an exciting bout, it hadn't drawn well, and Farr had been a clear loser so there was no great demand for a rematch. There was a lot written and said about how amazing it was that the Welshman had lasted the limit with Louis, and so the bout became one of the more memorable in Louis's career, and Farr became the only man who ever extended Joe that Joe did not take care of in a rematch before his retirement.

Farr returned to England. In January, he returned to New York to face former champion Braddock, but dropped the decision. It was Braddock's first fight since the Louis loss and it turned out to be the last fight of his career. Although a winner, he absorbed a lot of punishment and decided to retire while he still had his health and a good reputation. Braddock didn't ask for another fight with Louis, and Farr didn't get one.

Joe returned to Chicago and moved with Marva into an apartment house at 4320 South Michigan Avenue she had purchased for $15,000 and furnished with antiques.

On February 23, 1938, he fought for Jacobs at Madison Square Garden. With Joe on his side, Jacobs, with his 20th Century Sporting Club, was named by John Reed Kilpatrick to replace Jimmy Johnston as promoter at the Garden. Joe took care of Jacobs. He fought when he was asked to fight. He didn't argue about money. And Jacobs took care of Joe. When Joe had spent whatever he'd made in his last fight, Jacobs advanced him money on his next fight.

"He give me ten, twenty, thirty thousand whenever I asked for it and he never asked me no questions and never lectured me or nothing," Joe gratefully remembered later.

Maybe it would have been better if he had.

Joe's foe early in 1938 was Nathan Mann. He was a

Sitting with co-manager John Roxborough, Joe Louis watches poker-faced as ever as Max Schmeling defeats Harry Thomas in New York in a December, 1937, tuneup for a rematch with Louis.

good fighter and a hard hitter. He wasn't afraid of anyone. He took the fight to Joe and hurt him a couple of times in the first couple of rounds. But Joe, weighing 200 pounds for the first time, knocked him down once in the second round and three times in the third round and the last time Mann stayed down.

The fight drew a full house of just under 20,000 fans, but ticket prices were scaled low and drew a gross gate of just a little over $110,000. Joe picked up a little over $40,500 for his short night's work.

Then Jacobs took Joe to Chicago Stadium to meet Harry Thomas on the first of April. This one drew a little over 10,000 fans and a little under $50,000 and Joe settled for $16,600. Thomas was tough and it took Joe five rounds to finish him off, but Thomas wasn't in Louis's league.

Joe had to defend his title against the best, and the big match lay just ahead. Reluctantly, Schmeling agreed to a mere 20 percent for the chance to repeat his conquest of The Brown Bomber and the chance to regain his heavyweight title. The match was made for Yankee Stadium in June and Jacobs saw it as a million-dollar match.

It was the most eagerly awaited fight of that time.

SCHMELING II

The second Joe Louis–Max Schmeling boxing match was more than a heavyweight title fight, more even than a chance for the greatest fighter of the decade to avenge the only loss on his record. It was in its way a warning of war, the United States of America against Nazi Germany.

In the middle months of 1938 the world was beginning to wonder whether it was facing World War II. Within the year Adolf Hitler's Nazi Germany would ally itself with Benito Mussolini's Fascist Italy and march on neighboring nations.

Soon England would be at war and, within a few years, so would the U.S.A., drawn in by Hirohito's imperialist Japan.

By 1938 the United States was becoming more aware of Hitler's persecution of Jews as he sought a pure, white Aryan "master race." The dictator had walked out on the black American Jesse Owens's great triumphs in the Olympics in Berlin a few years earlier.

Hitler sent Schmeling messages of faith in his superiority and warned him to win for the glory of the Third Reich. The dark-haired, heavy-browed fighter was considered an ideal German. His manager and closest friend, Max Machon, was identified as a uniform-wearing member of the Nazi party. Machon said, "Schmeling will win for Germany." Schmeling said, "No colored boy can beat me. I will become the first to win back the heavyweight title."

Even at a time when blacks were being lynched in the South and white supremacists like the Ku Klux Klan were flourishing, a young Negro was being asked to win for his country. Whites who disliked "niggers" were rooting for The Brown Bomber. On a visit to the White House, Joe Louis had his arm felt by President Roosevelt, who told him, "We're depending on those muscles for America," a widely quoted comment.

While anti-Nazi groups picketed Schmeling's training camp in the Adirondack Mountains in upstate New York, crowds of 5,000 or more cheered Joe's training routines at his camp at Pompton Lakes, New Jersey. Jack Blackburn and Manny Seamon drilled Louis on keeping his left high and blocking right leads. Joe was skilled by now in the boxing sciences. If his feet were slow, his hands were fast. He boxed well behind his left jab and, of course, punched powerfully with either hand.

Some powerful punchers hit hard with one hand, but few ever hit as hard with either hand as Joe. His left jab was the hardest in history and he could, as few others ever could, knock out a man with one left hook, right cross, right uppercut, or straight right. He was accurate and did not waste punches. Blackburn always taught him that he didn't have to throw ten punches when one would do. He taught Joe to shuffle forward behind his jab, applying steady pressure to his rivals, looking for openings.

The speed of Joe's hands was such that he needed only a little opening. In the split second in which he saw one, a fist was flying through it to its target. He hurt anyone he hit. When he hurt someone, he usually finished him. Blackburn taught him to take his time and throw good punches when a foe was in bad shape. A Farr, an opponent he did not finish off fast, was a rarity.

Blackburn had been a bad guy a lot of his life. He'd been involved in deadly dealings with others. Early in his life he'd spent time in prison for a fatal assault. Even before Joe became champ he went to court with Blackburn as a character witness, helping to clear his trainer after a street fight in which one man was fatally shot and a little girl seriously wounded.

But Blackburn had been a brilliant boxer and he was a brilliant teacher of boxing. He loved Louis and taught him everything he knew about boxing. Supposedly slow-witted, Louis learned a lot. He was smart in the ring. His great talent could be used to its full extent. He loved his "Chappie" and listened to him and learned from him. By the middle of 1938, The Brown Bomber was at his peak and nobody in ring history may ever have been better.

He was surprisingly relaxed in training, yet he worked hard in heavy heat. Every morning he ran six miles. Blackburn and others would drive him to a point on the lake six miles from camp and ride back, relaxing in the car, while he ran back. Years later Joe recalled getting mad because they had it easy while he had it hard: "Ooohhh, it was hot! I'm doing six miles on the road and Blackburn is telling me, 'Chappie, it's nothing. You can do it easy.'

"One day, Blackburn and me and a couple of others take our ride to the end of the road, six miles. We're walking around and one of my sparring partners is out there in a boat, rowing around. The others are throwing rocks at him. I jump in the car and drive home. They run after me. I stay just ahead of them, so they can see the car. When they slow down, I slow down. I make 'em walk six miles," Joe laughs, slapping his leg and treasuring the memory of it. "That Blackburn, he died," Joe laughs.

The world was making a war of it, but to Joe it was just a fight, though one he wanted to win more than any other he had ever fought. He was sure he would win. He would not make the mistakes he'd made two years earlier to the month. He was not going to give the German a chance. The night before Joe left camp, he sat with the sportswriter Jimmy Cannon, talking about the bout.

"I'm betting you by a knockout in six rounds," Jimmy said.

Joe held up one finger. "It goes in one," Louis said.

The morning of the fight, June 22, 1938, Joe was awakened at nine by his bodyguard, Carl Nelson. No one needed a bodyguard less, except that Joe and his hands had to be protected from rough fans or crackpots. Joe dressed and drank a glass of orange juice. They left at ten, driving to the Athletic Commission office for the weigh-in at eleven.

There was a crowd waiting for him when he arrived. They cheered him. Police pushed him through. Schmeling was waiting. Joe weighed in at 198¾ pounds, Schmeling at 193 pounds. A large crowd of reporters pressed in on them. Flashbulbs popped as pictures were taken for the early editions of the newspapers. Joe and Max just nodded to each other. They did not speak to or insult each other.

Joe was taken to a friend's apartment on St. Nicholas Place. He sat around, rested, relaxed. Bill Bottoms fixed him a steak and salad and he ate at three. Then he took a walk with Blackburn and a friend, Freddy Wilson, along the Harlem River, near the Polo Grounds. Freddy asked him how he felt. Joe said, "I'm scared."

"Scared?" Wilson asked, surprised.

"Yeh, I'm scared I might kill him," Louis said, laughing.

They went back to the apartment and Joe lay down in the bedroom and napped. At seven they went to the stadium and Joe lay down on the dressing-room table and napped some more. At nine Blackburn awakened

Joe and started to bandage his hands. At nine-thirty Joe got up and shadowboxed for half an hour, three times as long as usual, harder than usual, loosening up more than usual, wanting to get a faster start than usual. At ten he walked down the tunnel, came up through the dugout, and walked down the aisle to the ring.

He remembered, later, "From the time I got to the stadium, there were cops wherever you looked. When we got to the stadium, you could hardly get in through the crowd. The cops pushed me through the people. In the dressing room, nobody made no jokes. This was serious business. It was an important fight.

"I warmed up until I was sweating good. I wanted to start like it was the third round. I was going to throw so many punches I wouldn't have had any left for the third round. No one expected that. They thought he was too good. They were there to see a good fight.

"When I got out of the dugout, I never saw so many people. They filled that place. I looked up and there were people as far up as I could see. They filled the chairs they'd put on the field, filling the infield and outfield. They jammed the aisles. The cops pushed me through. Never saw so many bluecoats. I needed 'em. They was all I needed."

There were more than 70,000 fans there. They had paid more than a million dollars to be there. Many had paid as much as $30 a ticket to be in the best seats, right behind the free rows of hundreds of sportswriters from all over the world and broadcasters who would send the action in English, German, and Spanish over radio around the globe. Some had paid more. Jacobs, the old hustler, had sold seats in the press section to many who were not members of the press for $200 each. Celebrities were everywhere. It was a spectacular affair.

Louis was a 9–5 favorite, but betting had been brisk. There were those who thought the 32-year-old veteran ex-champ was too smart for Joe, who had just turned 24. But Joe was cheered and Max was booed when the great ring announcer of the day, Harry Balogh, introduced the rivals.

Joe took off his silk blue and red bathrobe he always wore and a flannel robe he wore beneath it for warmth. Max took off the old gray robe he wore. Both had dark trunks on. Both looked fit as they moved about in their corners, waiting. Schmeling glared across the ring at his rival, but Joe was expressionless as usual.

At mid-ring, the great referee Arthur Donovan waited to work the scheduled 15-rounder. At ringside, the great American announcer Clem McCarthy and the German announcer, Arno Helmers, waited to broadcast the bout. Millions leaned close to radios around the world, waiting.

The outer lights went out. The crowd hushed. The bell rang. The rivals moved across the ring at one another in that dramatic, tense spotlight.

Louis moved right in on Schmeling, jabbing hard. Joe hooked a left to the body which made Max wince, then hooked a left to the head which snapped Schmeling's head back. Max backed up, but Joe moved in on him and drove a right to the jaw which sent Schmeling reeling into the ropes.

The crowd was standing and screaming already.

Max came off the ropes and threw a right hand, which was blocked, and a left jab, which was short. Joe hooked a hard left high on Schmeling's head and drove a straight right to Schmeling's jaw, which hurt him.

Eyes wide, Max moved along the ropes, backing away. Holding on to the top rope, he turned away from his tormentor as though that would stop him from hitting him. All Louis had to hit was Schmeling's back.

Joe ripped a right to Schmeling's side, but the brutal blow landed partly on the German's back. And Schmeling screamed in pain. No one who was there ever will forget it. The referee moved between the two, waved Louis to a neutral corner, and started to give Schmeling a standing count.

Schmeling moved away from the ropes while still hanging on to the top rope with his hand as though afraid to leave its safety. But there was no safe place for him in that ring. There was a look of fear in his dark eyes.

Louis sent a vicious left to the side of his head and smashed a right to his chin that sent Schmeling down, dazed. He didn't know what he was doing. He got up.

The crowd was hollering.

A member of the Third Reich radio crew pulled a plug, blacking out the broadcast of the bout back in

Germany. In the broadcast in this country, Clem McCarthy was growling excitedly, "Schmeling is up and Louis is on him."

Louis sent lefts and rights to his helpless foe so fast that McCarthy couldn't keep up with them. A left hook sent Schmeling down again.

The fans were near hysteria.

Schmeling struggled gallantly erect and Louis tore into him once more. A left hook to the head staggered the German, and a right cross to the side of his chin twisted his face into a look of awful agony. He crumpled from the knees and fell forward on his arms and face. He lay as though paralyzed.

Max Machon threw a towel into the ring, but this sign of surrender no longer was allowed. The referee kicked it onto the middle strand of ropes and bent over the German, counting.

At five, he finished. It was clear that Schmeling was unconscious, possibly seriously hurt. The referee waved his arms over the fallen fighter and the fight was finished at two minutes and four seconds of the first round.

Somebody later counted 50 punches thrown by Louis in the films of the first round, as long as it lasted. Schmeling threw only two. It remains the most savage, one-sided assault ever recorded by one man on another in the history of the ring. It is remembered as the most terrifying moment boxing has had. Louis is remembered more for that knockout than any other, and it is said that no man could have stood up to him that night.

Revenge belongs to The Brown Bomber as Max Schmeling falls in the first round of their rematch at Yankee Stadium, June, 1938.

Sequence shows the frightening power of Joe Louis's right-hand punch as it finishes Max Schmeling in the first round of their return bout. As referee Arthur Donovan strides away in the final photo, a white towel of defeat is thrown into the ring from Schmeling's corner.

1

It was sensational. It stunned the press and public who were there that night and all who listened to it on radio or later watched it on film. It triggered a series of near-riots across the country as blacks celebrated in New York, Chicago, Cleveland, Detroit, and elsewhere. It established Louis as the most frightening fighter of all time and avenged the only loss he ever suffered in his prime.

"It was a good fight," Joe said later in his quiet way.

"It didn't last long," a reporter reminded him as the press laughed.

"But it was good as long as it lasted," Joe said.

"When did you know you had him?" someone asked.

"When he signed for the fight," Joe said. And the writers laughed. They were beginning to see that Joe had a sense of humor and they really liked and respected him. He didn't brag and he didn't insult his foes, but he was straight with them.

Schmeling could not talk. He had to be helped from the ring and rushed to a hospital. He had suffered internal injuries and complained that he had been fouled by an illegal kidney punch. Joe said, "He didn't give me nowhere else to hit him."

Schmeling recovered and returned to Germany in disgrace. Still, he had been a champion. He never fought in the ring again, but he was allowed to fight for his country in World War II. Later, he and Joe met and became friends.

That night of June 22, 1938, in Yankee Stadium, 70,043 fans paid $1,015,012 to see little more than two minutes of action, but not a one of them ever regretted it and they talked about it from then on. It was an unforgettable fight.

The crowd was the third largest, the gate the second largest and Joe's purse of $349,228 the second largest of his entire career, but it was the frightening nature of his animal-like attack on his rival that would be best remembered, and it was beating the man who had beaten him that pleased him most.

"It was one of the great nights," Louis said later.

In the New York *Times*, James P. Dawson wrote, "The exploding fists of Joe Louis crushed Max Schmeling last night in the ring at Yankee Stadium and kept sacred the time-worn legend that no former heavyweight champion has ever regained the title.

"The Brown Bomber from Detroit, with the most furious early assault he has ever exhibited, knocked out Schmeling in the first round of what was to have been a 15-round battle. . . .

"The battle was short, but it was furious and savage while it lasted, packed with drama . . . For excitement, for pulse throbs, those who came from near and far felt themselves well repaid. They saw a fight that, though one of the shortest heavyweight championships on record, was surpassed by few for thrills. . . .

"Schmeling claimed he was fouled . . . The punches which dazed him were thundering blows to the head, jaw, and body in bewildering succession . . . No fighter ever was more thoroughly knocked out."

Joe Louis's career really was just beginning, his reign in heavyweight ring ranks just started, but he had reached a peak he never could top, having given what would be the most memorable performance of his life.

THE BUM OF THE MONTH CLUB

Joe Louis defended his heavyweight title once the year he won it. He defended it three times the first full year he held it, four times the second year, four times the third year, and seven times the fourth year, before he entered the service. In all, he defended it nineteen times in a little more than four years before he went into the Army, and he defended his title twice more while a soldier in the service.

By contrast, Jack Johnson defended his heavyweight title seven times in seven years and Jack Dempsey six times in seven years. Jess Willard defended twice in four years, Gene Tunney twice in two years, Max Schmeling twice in two years, and Jimmy Braddock once in two years. The heavyweights never had a fighting champion like Louis.

When you fight nineteen foes in four years or so, you take on anyone who has any claim at all on a title shot. All can't be outstanding. But Joe took 'em all on, logical contenders and lower-ranked challengers right through the ratings of the late 1930s. Almost all were dangerous.

They were heavyweights and most could hit. Joe took his chances.

After taking the title from Jimmy Braddock in June of 1937, Louis decisioned Tommy Farr in August, ten weeks later. In 1938, he knocked out Natie Mann in three rounds in February, Harry Thomas in five rounds in April, and Max Schmeling in one round in June. Following the emotional excesses of the Schmeling match, he did rest the remainder of the year.

In 1939 he went to work in earnest. Late in January he met John Henry Lewis, who was light-heavyweight champion although not recognized as such in New York State. Lewis had taken the title from Bob Olin in October of 1935 and defended it successfully five times in four years. He'd also beaten such heavyweights as Red Burman, Red Barry, Al Ettore, Johnny Risko and Braddock. He was an outstanding defensive fighter and a sharp puncher who, at the age of 34, had lost only seven of 104 fights and had 54 knockout victories.

There was considerable controversy about the bout. Joe had been the first black to get a heavyweight title shot in almost thirty years. Now he wanted to give another one a shot. He admired John Henry, who had blazed a bit of a trail for him, and had come to be his friend. Also, Joe knew what boxing officials did not know —that Lewis had lost most of the vision in his left eye.

Joe did not want to fight a friend, especially one who had a handicap. But John Henry, nearing the end of his career, wanted the fight, and Joe did not want to deprive

At 23, Joe Louis is barely out of breath after his title-fight knockout of Harry Thomas at Chicago in April, 1938. He sits in his dressing room, flanked by trainer Jack Blackburn, left, and co-manager Julian Black.

him of a big payday. They did not match blacks in big fights in those days, and Jacobs did not think the match would draw well, but Joe insisted that John Henry have his night.

An acceptable turnout of 17,338 showed up at the Garden, the gate was a little over $100,000, Joe earned a little under $35,000 and John Henry picked up almost $20,000 for what was to be his final fight.

Joe, who outweighed his friend by twenty pounds, knocked him down three times in the first round and Lewis was counted out at 2 minutes and 29 seconds of the round. A right hand that everyone saw but John Henry finished him. Later, Joe said, "I wanted to finish it fast. That way he didn't get hurt much. I don't like hitting no friend."

Joe met Jack Roper in Los Angeles's Wrigley Field, where baseball's minor league Angels played. There was a turnout of almost 22,000 fans and a gate of almost $90,000. Joe earned almost $35,000. Roper was a left-hander with a good left hook and Joe worried about that a bit, but flattened him at 2:20 of the first round with a right cross.

Afterward an announcer asked Roper what went wrong. Jack laughed and said, "I zigged when I should have zagged." Louis was sitting there, too, and he laughed, too. Roper was the third straight man Joe had knocked out in the first round, a record for heavyweight title fights. The three together had lasted less than seven minutes.

Next came one of Joe's most colorful foes, who made one of Joe's most spectacular fights. He was "Two-Ton" Tony Galento, who had a saloon in New Jersey and looked as if he drank most of the beer himself. He stood five-foot-nine and weighed 230 pounds. He had a homely face and a big belly. He had hair everywhere but on top of his head. Louis called him, "That funny little fat guy." A lot of people thought of Galento as a funny little fat guy, and didn't think he belonged in the ring with Joe.

But Galento was a barroom brawler with a big punch. He cut easily and bled a lot, but he had a lot of heart and was tough to stop. He lost 26 of 114 fights in his career, but he was only knocked out six times, and he knocked out 59 foes. He lost to Natie Brown, Ernie Schaaf, Arturo Godoy, Max Baer, and Buddy Baer, among others, but he knocked out Natie Mann and Red Barry, among others, and he'd flattened 11 foes in a row when he got a shot at Joe and the title.

Considered a clown, Galento kept saying, "I'll moider da bum!" There were newsreels of him training with a beer barrel, saying "I'll moider da bum!" He even telephoned Joe to tell him that. It became a popular saying at the time. Joe just laughed. But Tony was not to be laughed at. He was tough.

The novelty of the attraction lured almost 35,000 fans to Yankee Stadium and they paid $333,000 to be there, producing payoffs of almost $115,000 for Joe and $55,000 for Tony that June night in 1939, a year from the Schmeling match. The fans were not disappointed. Those who did not go, were.

Louis came out to put Tony away fast. Joe was careless. Tony came out of his crouch with a leaping left hook that caught Joe on the side of his jaw and staggered him. Galento followed with a right cross and left hook that hurt Joe. Later, Joe admitted, "My eyes glazed over." But Tony couldn't believe he'd hurt the champ. He studied Joe through his small eyes, hesitated, and didn't follow up.

Between rounds, a concerned Blackburn warned Joe to jab and box this guy and not take any chances with him. He was fat and sure to tire fast. But Joe was annoyed and angry. He moved in on the fat man, punching powerfully. He reopened old cuts on Galento's puffy face. Joe hit Tony with a right uppercut that lifted the 230-pounder right off his feet and dropped him right on his rear. But at the count of five, Tony was on his feet again and fighting back.

"I couldn't believe it. I never hit a man harder who got up. Any other man would've stayed down," Joe said later.

Louis went to finish Galento in the third round. "Two-Ton" Tony was easy to hit. Joe took target practice on the fat man with thunderous punches. Galento was bleeding from cuts around his eyes and in his mouth. He was bleeding from his nose. He was awful-looking. But he was street-tough. A leaping left hook caught Joe right on the jaw and dumped him on the seat of his pants.

The fans came to their feet shouting their surprise. The radio announcer shouted his surprise to stunned fans across the country. Joe was surprised, but not stunned. "I just felt foolish," he later remarked. Joe jumped right up and tore angrily into Tony. He stepped inside the fat man's wild punches and drove short, straight, punishing punches into Tony's face.

"Two-Ton" Tony Galento is a bloodied and open target for heavyweight champion Joe Louis's left hook seconds before referee Arthur Donovan stopped their June, 1939, match in the fourth round.

The bloody challenger reeled backward, taking a terrible beating bravely. He got through the third round and into the fourth before he fell, finally, from a left and right that all but tore his head off and left him crawling aimlessly on the floor. He was counted out at 2:29 of the round. Relieved, Louis left to cheers, but even bigger cheers were given Galento as he was helped away.

He may have been a buffoon, but he was brave. He hollered for a rematch, but he was the only one who wanted it. Others feared he'd be hurt terribly. Yet, three months later Tony knocked out Lou Nova, a ranking contender, in a bloody brawl. But the next year he was knocked out by Max Baer, still fighting for a living. And, the year after that, by Max's brother, Buddy. Galento laid off a couple of years, then came back. He knocked out his last seven foes before retiring in 1944.

He and Joe became friends. A lot of men who lost to Joe became his friend. It was no disgrace to lose to Louis. Joe was simple, straightforward, friendly. He used to go to Tony's saloon in New Jersey and they'd laugh about how Tony had surprised Joe. "I had ya, ya bum," Tony would say, and Joe would just laugh and admit, "Ya surely did."

In September, less than three months after the Galento brawl, Jacobs made a rematch for Louis with Bob Pastor at the Tigers' ballpark, Briggs Stadium, in Detroit. This was the first title defense for The Brown Bomber in his home town.

To give him extra time to catch the fast-footed former collegian, the match was set at 20 rounds. This was the first time a heavyweight title bout was set at 20 rounds since Jess Willard took the title from Jack Johnson in Havana in 1915. Dempsey and Tunney fought 10-rounders for the title, but since then the standard distance had been set at 15 rounds for title fights.

A superb boxer as well as fast on his feet, Pastor had

run the entire 10 rounds with Louis to make him look bad back in January of 1937, and some gave him a chance to outsmart and outbox Joe in September of 1939, less than three years later. The fight drew almost 34,000 fans who paid almost $350,000, and Joe's check was almost $120,000.

But it bothered Bob that he was ridiculed for running in their first fight, and he came out fighting. It was a mistake. He was floored five times in the first two rounds. But Joe didn't catch him with a knockout punch, and Bob went back on his bicycle. He ran and ran and ran and took a bloody beating until Louis caught him with a knockout punch in the 11th.

Braddock was there and the next morning Pastor spotted him at breakfast in the dining room of the Book-Cadillac Hotel. Stopping by Braddock's table, Bob said he was doing fine until a butt opened a cut over his eye and he got blood in his eyes and couldn't see. Braddock looked at Pastor, whose face cuts were covered with protective tape. Braddock laughed a little and said, "Yeah. Hits pretty good, don't he?"

Joe took the rest of the year off, but after a trip with his wife to Cuba, where he was met by President Batista, and after a trip home for the holidays, Joe returned to training for his first fight of 1940, with Arturo Godoy of Argentina early in February at the Garden.

Godoy was the heavyweight champion of South America. He had not lost in his first 39 fights and had lost only seven times in 68 fights through ten years in the ring. He campaigned in this country for a year or so and lost to Natie Mann and Roscoe Toles, but beat Tony Galento twice and knocked out Jack Roper.

Earlier, he split two fights with former light-heavyweight titleholder Tommy Loughran and knocked out former heavyweight contender Luis Angel Firpo, who knocked Dempsey out of the ring before being flattened in their wild title fight. Close to 30, Godoy was still tough and durable.

The fight drew more than 15,000 fans, but tickets were priced low and the gate was less than $90,000. Louis picked up less than $25,000. He had no enthusiasm for the fight.

He couldn't get to Godoy, who fought the entire fight from a low crouch, throwing only an occasional punch up at Joe. The champ pounded out a unanimous decision, but he couldn't put over a finishing punch on the Argentinian, who became the second challenger to last the limit with Louis.

Joe later reported, "This was the worst fight I ever had."

Not because he'd put up a good fight, but because he'd gone the distance, Godoy swiftly was booked for a rematch in Yankee Stadium in June. But first Louis took on Johnny Paychek of Chicago back in New York's Garden in March. Paychek had been knocking out everyone he fought in the Midwest, but he seemed to freeze from fear in his fight with Louis. "He just seemed scared," Louis said later. About 10,000 fans saw Joe take out Johnny in two rounds, picking up about $20,000 of a $60,000 gate.

In June, more than 26,000 fans paid almost $165,000 to see Louis pick up $56,000 getting Godoy in eight rounds of their rematch. Godoy continued his tactics of crouching, but Joe jabbed down at him with fearful force until the South American was bleeding badly from cuts above both eyes. Joe floored him in the sixth, but the bell saved him. Joe knocked him down twice in the eighth and referee Billy Cavanaugh stopped the slaughter.

Godoy came back to this country later in the year to outpoint good fighters like Gus Dorazio and Tony Musto. He continued to fight for seven more years, splitting his time between this country and his country. He defeated some fine fighters and won most of his fights before his 17-year career came to an end. Near the end he boxed exhibition bouts with Joe in Mexico and Chile and they, too, became friends.

Godoy fought a black American, Roscoe Toles, seven times in South America in the early 1940s and beat him only once, but Toles had more trouble with other fighters and, what with a decline in Louis's activity while he was in service during the war years, was one of the few qualified fighters who did not get a shot at Joe's title.

Following Godoy, Louis took some time off to have a good time. But war had begun in Europe, and the United States had begun to draft and train young men for war. The 26-year-old Louis had registered for the draft, and he went on an exhibition boxing tour of training camps to entertain the recruits.

Returning to real action in December, he made his first appearance in Boston, at the Boston Garden, and drew 13,0000 fans and a gate of $50,000 for his 12th defense of his title, against Al McCoy. He pounded the Irishman into submission in six rounds. It was worth a little under $18,000 to Joe, who was spending his money as fast as he made it and had to keep on fighting.

This started what Jack Miley of the New York *Post* termed "The Bum of the Month Club"—referring to the opponents Louis put away—and the phrase became famous, symbolic of Joe's pace in those days.

The following month Joe knocked out Red Burman in five rounds before 18,000 fans in New York's Madison Square Garden. The next month, less than three weeks later, Joe knocked out Gus Dorazio in two rounds before 15,000 fans in Philadelphia's Convention Hall. The next month he stopped Abe Simon in 13 rounds before 16,000 fans in Detroit's Olympia. The month after that, he took out Tony Musto in nine rounds before 17,000 fans at the St. Louis Arena. And the month after that, he stopped Buddy Baer before almost 25,000 fans outdoors in Washington, D.C.'s Griffith Stadium.

They may not have been great fighters but they were really not bums, and Louis several times had less than three weeks between bouts.

Fighters seldom are flattened by body punches, but Louis stopped Burman with a left hook to the belly that the great writer Red Smith later said was the fiercest single punch he ever saw. A left hook to the head did in Dorazio and he later said he hurt for two weeks. Musto boxed brilliantly to keep Louis at bay for a while, but later he admitted he never forgot the short right that ruined his game effort.

Simon was a monster of a man and he wanted and was granted a 20-rounder, feeling he could wear down and outlast Louis. The six-foot-five, 255-pound Simon did lean on Joe, did wear him down some, did land some good punches in his awkward way, and did take some good punches, but he didn't last and gave way from a barrage of blows in the 13th round.

The scoring, revealed later, did cause a bit of controversy. The referee, Hennessy, did have Joe an easy winner by 9 rounds to 2 with 1 even at the end. One judge, Neville, had Joe in front by 7 rounds to 4 with 1 even. The controversy came from the other judge, Butler, who had Louis in front in rounds 3 to 1 with 8 even.

"You never know how those guys gonna figure a fight, which is why it was best to win by knockout. A lot of men lost titles on bad decisions," Louis said later.

Baer was another monster of a man. Older brother Max was a better boxer, but younger brother Buddy was bigger and braver. The six-foot-six, 235-pound Buddy had a big punch and landed a long left hook to the side of Louis's face in the first round that sent Louis stumbling backward and sprawling through the ropes. Landing on the apron of the ring just above press row, he got to his knees and then climbed between the ropes and back into the ring by the count of four.

"I was surprised and confused, but not groggy," Louis later recalled. The crowd, which included many leading political figures in the nation's capital, was surprised, too —on its feet and hollering for an upset by Baer, who was, like many of Joe's foes at the time, a 20–1 underdog.

Schmeling, Braddock, Galento, and now Buddy Baer had floored Louis. Getting knocked down was not the mark of a great fighter. But getting up to win was. Clearly, Louis did not take a punch too well. But he took it well enough to recover from one fast. Except for the Schmeling match, Louis was not knocked out, and he survived several knockdowns that night. He had been knocked down a lot, but knocked out only the one time.

Now he got back up and battled back, battering Baer the rest of the round and all the second round. But Baer was strong and durable and he fought back in the third, forcing Joe to the ropes with a barrage of right-hand blows. Joe was bruised over his left eye, which started to swell. In the fourth, Baer went toe-to-toe with Louis and forced him to hold on and clinch at one point. And in the fifth a left-handed punch by Baer tore open a cut under Louis's left eye.

Angrily Louis stormed back, battering Baer and staggering him with heavy hits before the bell ended the session, which had the fans in an uproar. Starting the sixth, Louis stormed into his enormous foe, who towered over him and outweighed him more than 35 pounds.

Both hands battered Baer badly. Desperately the brave Baer tried to battle back, standing toe to toe with Louis and slugging with him. But a frightening right hand dumped him.

Baer was hurt terribly, but somehow he staggered to his feet at seven. Louis sailed into him, both hands flying, and the big guy gave way again, going down heavily on his back. It was near round's end and all was madness in that arena. Baer rolled onto his stomach and sought to push himself up, but it didn't look as if he could make it. At about the time referee Arthur Donovan counted, "nine, ten," Baer arose and Louis slugged him down again as the bell rang.

It wasn't clear whether Baer had beaten the ten-count or Louis, with his last blow, had beaten the bell. Joe's friend, Freddie Guinyard, dashed into the ring to congratulate Louis on his victory, but, finding out the fight was not yet over, dashed right out again. Donovan waved him away and went to Joe to tell him the fight was still on. Meanwhile, Baer had been helped to his corner and was being worked on by trainer Ray Arcel and second Izzy Kline while manager Ancil Hoffman came out of the corner to protest to Donovan that Louis had hit Baer after the bell.

In the enormous noise in the ballpark, nobody had heard the bell. Donovan tried to explain that to Hoffman, but Hoffman didn't want to listen.

As the bell rang to start the seventh round, Louis came uncertainly out of his corner and stood at mid-ring, ready to resume, but Baer remained seated and Hoffman stood in front of him, demanding that Donovan award the bout to Baer because a foul punch had left him unable to continue.

By the rules, Hoffman being in the ring was a foul in itself. Twice, Donovan ordered Hoffman to leave the ring. Twice, Hoffman refused. Baer remained in his corner. Donovan walked over to Louis, raised his hand, and declared him the winner on a foul.

Thus the ending was controversial, although almost all felt Louis had defeated Baer fairly and few felt Baer could continue. It is generally regarded as a knockout, although the *Ring Record Book* lists it as a foul.

In the next day's New York *Times*, Joseph C. Nichols wrote, "Joe Louis was successful in the seventeenth defense of his heavyweight championship of the world when he defeated the ponderous Buddy Baer in Griffith Stadium . . .

"The bare statement of the champion's victory, however, falls far short of conveying the drama, excitement, surprise, and uncertainty of a contest that contained more thrills than any heavyweight title bout since the oft-referred-to classic between Jack Dempsey and Luis Angel Firpo in 1923.

"Arthur Donovan, who refereed tonight's clash, named Louis the winner on a foul in the seventh round, but before the bell sounded for the last official session the fans in the ball yard had been treated to the spectacle of Joe Louis on the floor, Joe Louis out of the ring, Joe

Louis holding, Joe Louis clinching, and Joe Louis bleeding.

"In addition, they had also seen the towering Baer absorb an unbelievable amount of punishment in his own right, punishment that reached its culmination in the sixth round when he was sent sprawling to the canvas three times. . . . The unusual ending and the award were satisfactory to the fans, and they applauded roundly. They seemed to realize that the fight could produce no further thrills comparable to those they already had seen."

Louis was worn out. He had defended his championship six times in six months. He was making money, but he was wearing down.

The McCoy, Burman, Dorazio, Simon, and Musto bouts had drawn gates of from $50,000 to a little above $60,000 each. Joe had drawn purses of from $17,000 to a little above $22,000 from each. The Baer gate topped $100,000 and Joe's share topped $35,000. In the preceding six months, Joe had earned close to $170,000 for a series of fights with lightly regarded rivals. He had another fight scheduled the following month that figured to make him about that much in one night, for his foe was the highly regarded light-heavyweight champion, Billy Conn, and promoter Mike Jacobs was looking for a half-million-dollar match at the Polo Grounds.

But Joe was too tired and had taken too much punishment without time to recuperate to be at his peak, while Billy Conn was a brilliant boxer and daring rival who was ready to give The Brown Bomber all he could deal with in what was to be one of the classic contests in the history of sports.

CONN I

The Billy Conn bout in June of 1941 was Joe Louis's 18th title defense in the two years almost to the day since he had won the heavyweight title, and his seventh in seven months. He'd knocked out 16 of the 18, more than half of them in five rounds or less, and he'd knocked out all of his last seven, but he had taken some punishment, he was tired, and he'd lost some of his enthusiasm for fighting.

Billy Conn was a brilliant boxer. He'd lost eight of 67 bouts, but five of those losses had come in his first year in the ring as a professional. He'd lost only three of his last 54 fights, and those to Young Corbett, Teddy Yarosz, and Solly Krieger, who were among the best boxers at a time there were many skillful fighters in the middleweight and light-heavyweight ranks.

Billy had beaten all in rematches. He also outboxed such standouts as Fritzie Zivic and Fred Apostoli, who, along with Krieger, had been or would be champions. He took the light-heavyweight championship from Melio Bettina in July of 1939 and successfully defended it once against Bettina and twice against Gus Lesnevich, a future champ, before giving it up in 1940 to campaign as a heavyweight.

In 1939, sportswriter Jack Miley, who had dubbed Joe Louis's run of victims "The Bum of the Month Club," wrote, "Not so long ago a skinny middleweight, William David Conn is growing like a weed. Now he's a light-heavyweight, the champion of his class. When he cleans up on those boys—and it won't be long—he will pick on Bob Pastor and any of the heavyweights who stand in his way. They won't hit him enough to hurt him. . . .

"By 1941 Louis will be even more jaded from fighting all the bums. And Conn will astound with his fearlessness, his speed. Heigh-ho, it is written in the cards, mates."

This prediction proved to be so accurate as to be unbelievable. Billy Conn had cleaned up on the light-heavyweight class, gone on to beat Bob Pastor, Al McCoy, Gus Dorazio, Lee Savold, and other ranking heavyweights, and by 1941 was about to astound Joe Louis with his boxing, bravery, and speed. He had won 19 in a row, the last four by knockouts. Although primarily a skillful stylist who was hard to hit, he had developed punching power.

At 174 pounds, Conn came into the Louis bout more than 25 pounds lighter than Louis, but he was faster than Joe. At 199½ pounds, Joe had trained down below 200 for the first time in a year in an effort to be quicker, but it cost him strength. Usually favored by from 10 to 1 to 20 to 1, Louis was only a 3–1 favorite for this one and Conn was considered the new "white hope." But few really expected the handsome, cocky Irishman to dazzle Louis.

It was sufficient an attraction that there were 54,487 fans filling the New York Giants' Polo Grounds that night of June 18 and, as described in our opening chapter, they saw a classic contest, one of the finest fights and best-remembered bouts in ring history, one which kept all who saw it or listened to it in a state of high excitement from the first moment when those two moved out under the spotlights in that darkened arena.

It was a classic confrontation between boxer and puncher. Although a good boxer with a lethal left jab, Louis lacked the foot speed to keep up with the dancing tactics of Conn, who kept moving in and out, side to side, ducking punches, blocking punches, punching sharply. Shuffling forward relentlessly, Louis's fast hands found Conn from time to time, and his punches shook Conn from time to time, but for a long time Billy took it and battled back.

Joe opened up as if he would bomb Billy because Conn was overcautious. About the third round, Billy began to box brilliantly, reaching his rhythm. In the fifth, Louis found Conn with a left hook to the jaw that staggered him, but Conn covered up and avoided being hit cleanly by the following barrage of blows. By the middle of the fight, Louis was frustrated and tiring, and Conn was gaining confidence and coming on.

All was bedlam in the ballpark as Conn carried the fight to Louis through most of the second half of the fight. He was cut and bleeding, but when he hurt Joe with left hooks and straight rights to the head near the end of the 12th round, Billy looked like a winner and began to think about winning big—by knockout instead of by decision.

Although it is remembered that way, it is not true that Conn only had to keep away from Louis to win a decision. In New York, the voting is by rounds. The scorers also award points. If the rounds come out even, the points are used. After 12 rounds judge Marty Monroe had Conn ahead, 7–4–1. Referee Eddie Joseph had him ahead 7–5. But judge Jim Healy had it 6–6.

Even on Monroe's card, Louis could still win by sweeping the last three rounds, provided he had picked up an edge in points. Conn had to win at least one of the last three rounds on two of the scorecards to clinch a decision. But he was winning rounds with his boxing at that point and did not have to go for a knockout to win.

That was his mistake. The challenger had survived some toe-to-toe punching with the champion and thought the champ was too tired and dazed to stand up to sharp punches, but he simply had not been nailed by one of Joe's best punches. In the 13th round Conn opened up and gave Louis an opening. Moving under a long left hook, Louis shot a right to the head that hurt terribly.

Less than a minute was left, but that was all Louis needed. As the fans went wild, Joe moved in for the finish. He hit Billy with a left hook and a right to the chin that sent him senseless to the canvas. There were two seconds left in the round when Conn was counted out. Winner and loser both were cheered as they left the ring, but Louis still was champion.

All the stories after that were about how close Conn had come. All the sympathy went to Billy. He took it in good humor. He said later, "I was a wise guy. I had him and I let him get away. If I hadn't hurt him in the twelfth and tried to knock him out in the thirteenth, I'd have beat him. If the bell had saved me in the thirteenth, I'd have wised up and never have let him hit me again. I'd still have won. But I made a mistake and I paid for it."

He laughed and added, "I'm just too Irish and too cocky for my own good."

The fact is, it is hard to fight 15 rounds without making a mistake, and Joe's foes paid heavily for their mistakes. The best boxer in the business at that time and one of the most superb boxing stylists of all time could not avoid Joe's bombs for 15 rounds. And Joe's ability to win with a punch or two or three when he was worn out from a grueling schedule and hurt from a hard fight made Louis seem more magnificent than ever.

As Louis himself said, "It doen't mean much to beat

nobodies. Beating good men is what makes you the best." For all of his lack of education and polish, Joe, in his simple way, spoke a lot of truth.

Jack Blackburn taught him that he didn't have to waste ten punches when one would do. Joe, himself, knew that he didn't have to waste a hundred words when ten would do.

Billy later laughingly asked Joe, "When I had the title won, how come you wouldn't let me keep it for about six months before you took it back?"

Joe asked right back, "How you gonna keep the title for six months when you couldn't keep it for three rounds?"

And Billy laughed. Billy said later, after their careers were complete, "I'm proud Joe and I are real close friends. He's a nice guy and never knocks anybody. He was the best and I know it and he knows it.

"He fought because he was the best and wanted to make a buck, but money never mattered to him. If he made a million bucks a month he'd blow it on craps or golf or give it away. I was with him once when a guy bummed a hundred off him. I asked Joe why he didn't just give him a twenty. Joe said, 'What's the difference? I'm going to lose it anyway.' "

Joe earned just under $153,000 for beating Billy. There was immediate demand for a rematch, which was certain to have a million-dollar gate, maybe twice as much, and earn Louis maybe as much as half a million. But two days after the fight, Germany and Italy closed the American consulates in their countries and ordered out all American representatives. War was on its way and it got in the way of another Louis–Conn contest.

Louis already had another title defense scheduled, against Lou Nova. It was put off to September. Nova was a tough fighter who beat most of the best. He also was a colorful character who attracted a lot of attention by talking about practicing Yoga and developing a "cosmic punch" which would "knock out Louis." This and Joe's close call against Conn attracted more than 56,000 fans to the Polo Grounds.

Joe said, "He can cosmic-punch me all he wants, but he better do it fast because the good old left-right combination punch gonna be hard for him to handle." A left to the head and right to the chin knocked Nova down near the end of the fifth round. He wobbled to his feet at the count of nine, but was unable to answer the bell for the sixth.

Louis collected just under $200,000 out of a close to $600,000 gate, and he needed every penny of it. He was falling into debt, though he was still spending his money freely.

Less than 10 weeks after the Nova fight, on December 7, 1941, the Japanese attacked Pearl Harbor and America was drawn into World War II. Louis and Conn soon were drafted into the service, and negotiations for their eagerly awaited rematch, worth a considerable amount of money to both, were postponed indefinitely.

"We both wanted it," Louis said later. "We were ready

and would have been at our peaks. It might have been as big as anything boxing has had. But the war got in the way and that was a lot more important."

Since neither served under fire, it's a loss to sports history that they did not meet then, when they were at their best, but both soon were in uniform and out of serious ring training and no longer ready for such a serious confrontation.

The life of Joe Louis entered a new stage and his career started to turn downward. Of course, he was not the only athlete to lose a lot of his best years to service in wartime, and he was lucky he was not one of the few who had to fight at the front and risk losing his life.

THE WAR YEARS

As 1941 turned into 1942, America was at war and Joe Louis was due to be drafted. Although the cost of a war in loss of life is almost too much to endure, the money spent on arming men to fight wars always brings prosperity to the home front, providing well-paid jobs for those who remain at home.

The heavyweight champion of the world, however, was broke. At a time when money was worth four times what it is today, he had earned more than a million dollars in title fights and spent more than he had earned. He owed promoter Mike Jacobs $60,000 in advances against his next purse.

One time when Mike was on his way out of town, Joe offered to drive him to the airport. Because Mike's arms were full, Joe offered to carry his coat in the terminal. At the gate, Joe asked for $10,000. Mike wrote him a check, laughed, and said, "For ten grand, I would have carried my own coat."

Joe lost $50,000 before he had to fold his softball team. He lost $25,000 when he opened and folded a restaurant, The Chicken Shack, in Detroit. He lost $100,000 when he opened and closed a night club, The Rhum-boogie, later renamed Swingland, in Chicago. He lost track of other investments, which went bad. He gave away or lent and never got back maybe as much as $100,000.

He spent hundreds of thousands on his wife, girl friends, and family. He paid hundreds of thousands in taxes, but when his accountant told him he was close to $100,000 in debt to the government he was advised to let it mount up until it was so much the authorities would settle with him for a lot less. It was the worst advice he ever got.

Knowing he was running around and seldom home, Marva sued him for divorce and asked for half the money he'd made and half the money he'd make in the future. He pleaded with her to give him another chance. She did, but he couldn't change.

They reconciled and during the war years she gave birth to their first child, a daughter he named Jacqueline in honor of Jack Blackburn, but Joe wasn't home for the birth. By the end of the year, she did divorce him and received a fourth of his future earnings, as well as considerable property. They sold their horse farm to the government, which made a state park of the property.

Louis had dined with President Roosevelt at the White House, but in 1940 he campaigned for the Republican candidate, Wendell Willkie, because John Roxborough's brother, a politician, convinced Joe that

Willkie would do more for blacks. Democrat Roosevelt won election to a third term, legal at that time. Willkie introduced Louis in the ring as "a great American" when Joe defended his title against Buddy Baer in January of 1942 for the benefit of the Navy Relief Fund.

It was a generous gesture by Joe, who took only $65,000 from the gate of just under $190,000, and used that to pay almost $50,000 in taxes. He had expenses of almost $50,000 in training camp costs and went into the hole on that. He risked his title without return for a good cause.

The fight drew almost 17,000 fans to Madison Square Garden. Baer had knocked down Louis and given him a good fight in their first fight. But Joe determined to end their rematch early. Jack Blackburn was sick. Before the fight, he told Joe he didn't think he could work his corner: "My heart's bad. I don't think I can climb those stairs."

Joe told him, "You won't have to climb them but once, Chappie." Baer landed left hooks early, but Louis landed a right hand to the chin of his 250-pound foe that knocked down the big man late in the opening round. Baer got up and Louis landed a left hook that knocked him down again. Baer got up again, but he was in bad shape and referee Frank Fullam stopped the fight with four seconds to go in round one.

Before the fight, Louis was called on to speak at a Navy Relief dinner. He spoke only a few words, but ended by saying, of the war, "We can't lose because we're on God's side." Afterward, buddy Billy Rowe, the writer, said, "You dummy, you got it wrong. You should have said, 'We're going to win because God's on our side.'" The next day, newspaper stories praised Joe for his comment and his saying became well known. Louis asked Rowe, "Who's the dummy now?"

Asked why he would fight for nothing, Joe said, "I ain't fighting for nothing, I'm fighting for my country."

After the fight, Joe was drafted into the Army. He did not ask for a delay or try to get out of it, although many athletes did. He figured he'd set a good example for all healthy young men. After he was sworn in, the New York *Times* called him "a championship citizen."

An army of photographers and newsmen witnessed his swearing-in and were waiting for him when he reported to Camp Upton, Long Island. Afterward, however, they were sent away and he was sent into basic training. He learned to take care of his uniform and rifle, he learned to march and drill, he learned to shoot and dig foxholes. He did all the dirty work of any recruit. He was special, he stood out among the others in his company, but he tried to be one of the boys.

The Army offered to send him to officer's training school, but Joe figured that with his lack of education he would not do well, and he worried that he had no right to lead men into battle. The Army decided that he would be of more use to them fighting in the ring than in battle. He had defended his title once for the

Navy Relief Fund, so the Army asked him to defend it again for the Army Relief Fund. Joe said he would.

Jacobs set up another rematch with another giant, Abe Simon, for March in Madison Square Garden. The gate was a little less than $150,000 and Joe took less than $50,000 for taxes. The Army took care of his training costs at a gym at Fort Dix, New Jersey. Blackburn was too ill to work with Joe, so Manny Seamon took over. Thousands of soldiers watched his workouts and several thousand attended the fight with tickets Joe purchased out of his own pocket. There were more than 15,000 fans at the fight.

Simon had lasted 13 rounds with Louis the last time, but Joe floored his 255-pound foe in the second, fifth, and sixth rounds, with the right-left combination finishing the big guy in 16 seconds of the sixth. He dedicated the victory to "Chappie," but a few weeks later had to ask for a furlough to attend Blackburn's funeral.

The trainer had died, finally, of a heart attack, and he was buried before a big crowd in Chicago. Joe cried for his friend and later admitted, "I knew my life and my fighting would never be the same without Chappie."

They tried to arrange a rematch with Billy Conn, who also was in the service by then, but Jacobs really didn't want to turn the kind of money that fight would make over to the Army Relief Fund. He agreed to do it and the fighters actually went into training for it, but Jacobs said he had to get the $60,000 Louis owed him and

$30,000 Conn owed him and other money out of the gate and the brass got mad and canceled the contest.

After that, Joe and Billy were asked to box or referee exhibition bouts at Army bases to build morale among the troops. They did not box one another, but at times traveled together. Once when a plane had to circle Liverpool, England, with a stuck landing gear, Conn moved in close to Louis and said, "Joe, I want to stick close to you. You were always a lucky guy." Louis just laughed. And they got down safely.

Louis also toured the Pacific Northwest and Alaska with the great referee Ruby Goldstein, who had been a fine fighter, and this country and Europe with Sugar Ray Robinson, whom he'd known as a youngster in Detroit and who was just about to come into his own as a fighter himself.

One day at the Army bus station at Camp Sibert, Alabama, Joe and Ray were hassled by some military police for sitting on a "whites only" bench. They refused to move and were arrested by the MP's. They were freed immediately because it was an embarrassment to the Army. The incident received wide publicity and "whites only" facilities at Army bases were abolished.

It is easily forgotten how bigoted and segregated the Armed Forces were during World War II, and not only in the South. There were "colored" divisions and separate facilities everywhere. Few blacks got an opportunity to advance in rank, although they got plenty of chances to advance at the front and get killed. In the

Navy, blacks were used almost exclusively as cook's helpers and kitchen help.

When, early in his service duty, Joe Louis was assigned to the cavalry at Fort Riley, Kansas, he met Jackie Robinson, who had been a great all-around athlete at UCLA and would, after the war, become the first black big-league baseball player. Robinson complained that he was not allowed to play for the military base's football or baseball teams. Louis went to the top and told a general he'd raise hell if blacks weren't permitted to play. They received permission.

Joe was not normally a crusader, but in the service he encountered bigotry he was not used to and it made him mad. His prominence and popularity made him welcome almost anywhere; this plus the publicity he commanded gave him a lot of power. When Robinson and other blacks could not get into officer's training school, Joe called Truman Gibson, a black lawyer from Chicago who was acting as an adviser to the Army on racial affairs. Robinson and others got in and became officers. When Louis later allied himself with Jim Norris and the International Boxing Club, Gibson became a key member of the club.

Joe had a soft time in the service. He even spent six months in Hollywood during the filming of Irving Berlin's musical *This Is the Army*. Joe did box close to 100 exhibition bouts and traveled close to 100,000 miles putting on shows for the troops. He was away from his career for 46 months. But he never really came under fire. The war ended in August and when Joe was discharged in October, 1945, as a sergeant with the Legion of Merit medal, he was 31 years old and had not had a real fight for three and a half years.

CONN II

When Joe Louis came out of the Army near the end of 1945, he owed the government more than $100,000 in back taxes and interest penalties, he owed Mike Jacobs $60,000, and he owed John Roxborough $40,000. But Roxborough, who had advanced Joe money during the champ's Army years, was in prison on conviction of running numbers.

Roxborough's contract calling for 25 percent of Joe's ring earnings still was valid. But a 10-year contract with Julian Black for another 25 percent of his earnings had expired and Joe did not renew it. Instead, he named Marva one of his "managers" and turned the 25 percent over to her as alimony.

Later, he reconciled with and remarried Marva, and in the spring of 1947 she gave him a son, Joseph Louis Barrow, Jr., nicknamed "Punchie." But she kept her 25 percent and spent her share of The Brown Bomber's earnings before they were divorced again in 1949.

Louis hired Marshall Miles to manage him for 10 percent. Miles was a black man from Buffalo whom Joe had met through Roxborough and Julian Black, and Joe had to have someone to negotiate for him. Mike Jacobs set up the rematch with Conn and it made close to $2 million—$1,925,564, to be exact, Joe's best-ever gate. Joe made $625,916, by far his best-ever purse. But Roxborough, Miles, and Marva took 60 percent of that. Joe owed Jacobs $150,000 by then and Mike took that. Training expenses took $50,000. There wasn't a lot left, and taxes still had to be paid.

Joe lived off Jacobs while he went back into training. He went on an exhibition tour of California and the Pacific Northwest late in 1945 and returned to Pompton Lakes for heavy workouts early in 1946. The eagerly awaited rematch with Billy Conn was scheduled for June 19 in Yankee Stadium. Jacobs set an unprecedented price of $100 for ringside seats and his ringside seats were laid out almost as far as the eye could see. He scared off a lot of customers. He predicted a gate of $3 million and fell far short. The turnout of 45,266 fans was almost 10,000 less than for the first fight.

Still, it was a big night in the old ballpark. Joe was 32 and Billy was 28. Neither had fought for 50 months. Neither took a tuneup fight. Both had lost a lot of speed, but Billy depended on speed far more than Joe. Joe was up to 207 pounds and Billy to 187 pounds, but Joe still had a lot more punching power than Billy. Going in, no one knew how much either had left. Everyone remembered their fantastic first fight. There was a lot of excitement in the stadium when Louis came down the aisle in his blue and red robe with a white towel draped over his head and Conn came down in green silk.

The first bell brought tense anticipation from the fans, but as the rounds started to pass without much happening the crowd grew restless. In the first round, Louis threw a hard punch and Conn clinched and muttered through his mouthpiece, "Hey, take it easy, Joe, we got fifteen rounds to go," and Joe laughed. They were old friends and the old fire had died down in both.

Neither could do what he wanted to do in there and they struggled with one another, round after round, until the fans began to boo. A right to the chin staggered Conn in the fifth round, but he didn't go down and Louis couldn't catch Conn to finish him off. That in itself was the tipoff that Louis had lost something. At the midway point, the fans were restless and booing the boxers.

But before the bell for the eighth round, Louis told his second, Manny Seamon, "I'm gonna go out and go for it and see if he can take it." Midway in the round he reached Billy with a right to the head that opened a cut above Billy's left eye. A right to the jaw staggered Conn. Suddenly, it was the good old days. Louis was making magic again. The fans were standing and hollering at him to finish his foe. Louis landed another right to the head that shook Conn. Then a left hook to the jaw that knocked Conn unconscious. Lying on his back, he was counted out. And the crowd cheered Joe as if he were the Joe of old.

In the New York *Post*, Jimmy Cannon wrote, "It

ceased to be sport when Louis let the big right go, then another right, and then the left hook as Conn fell off the rim of the conscious and crumpled into the dark privacy of the night. . . . It was like watching a friend of yours being run over by a trolley car, watching it coming and knowing what would happen, but looking at it quietly, the curiosity dominating the horror. . . . Maybe it was sudden, but it was there all the time, the knockout inevitable. . . .

"They seemed fascinated by each other and appeared to be admiring each other's style instead of going about the job they were paid to do. . . . I saw the puckers of fat where Louis's arms join his shoulders, and his stomach moved when his legs did as though it were not part of him but a slab of meat tied around his waist . . . Conn danced . . . Billy bluffed with his hands . . . It became obvious that Joe was waiting and Conn was running. . . . Everyone knew the big man was coming on and the little man was going.

"The finish came unexpectedly because it destroyed a man, but not suddenly because Conn was always the hunted, who escaped only temporarily from the trap. The right, the right again, and the left against the jaw of the falling man. He was on his back, the blood running all over him, the referee counting . . ."

In his dressing room, surrounded by reporters and with the flashbulbs of the cameramen popping, Joe was described as dignified and calm, not gloating, but trying to tell it as it had happened: "I told my corner it was time to go out and see if I could still fight and he could still take it. He was a better fighter the first time."

Conn said, "We were both better fighters five years ago. We lost a lot."

He was asked, "When did he hurt you?"

He said, "When he hit me," and his battered face broke into a big grin.

"Are you going to fight again?"

"As lousy as I was, I should re-enlist in the Army," Conn laughed.

It was gone and he knew it, the chance to be heavyweight champ. He'd almost had the crown five years earlier, but he never came close this night, and now it was too late. He did not fight again for two years, tried again, won a couple of fights from mediocre foes, felt he could never recapture the old skills, and gave it up for good.

But Louis had to go on. He said later, "I was still the champ and I still needed dough. I was ready to retire, but I needed dough. I was so busy paying back bills, I couldn't get a few bucks put aside for my old age. After the Conn fight, my first fight out of service, I knew I'd lost a lot. I didn't know if I'd lost it to the years in the Army or just to the years. I thought maybe I was rusty and would get it back. I had to go on."

Mike Jacobs made a match for Joe with Tami Mauriello at Yankee Stadium in September. Tami was a young comer with a big punch. The fight drew almost 40,000 fans and, at lower rates, $335,000. Joe made more than

$100,000, but, as usual, he got less than half of that and, after the bills were paid, got to keep little of it. It was always the same. He risked a lot and wound up with little to show for it.

Mauriello landed a left hook to Louis's jaw and a right cross to his head in the first round that sent the champ staggering into the ropes and brought the crowd shouting to its feet. Throwing caution to the winds, Tami stormed at the old man. Mauriello was wide open. A hurt, angry Louis stepped in and hammered Mauriello. Tami went down, got up, got hit, went down again, got up again, got hit again, went down again, and didn't get up.

He was counted out at 2:09 of the first round, a record fifth championship-fight first-round KO for Louis and the tenth first-round KO of his incredible career. It also was his last.

"That was the last time I felt like my old self, but only because Mauriello made me mad and gave me the opening," Louis said later. "When I got back to my apartment building there was a crowd waiting to cheer me and I thought to myself I'd still be back there in the ring fighting if he hadn't hit me hard and made me mad and come at me like he had nothing to fear."

In his dressing room, a disappointed Tami Mauriello laughed a little and said sadly into an open microphone, "I just got too goddam careless." His slip went out to the radio audience and made him famous forever. The fact was, you couldn't afford to get careless even with a fading Joe Louis.

WALCOTT I & II

Joe Louis started to think about retiring after the rematch with Billy Conn. He was 34 years old and he'd lost a lot. All he was gaining was weight. Training no longer was fun for him. He hated to get up early in the morning to run. He dreaded the heavy work. He was bored by sparring. After Tami Mauriello, Joe didn't fight for more than a year. Except exhibitions. He went to California, Hawaii, Havana, Panama, Mexico, San Salvador, Chile, and Colombia to box exhibitions and make some money. Deep in debt, he still needed money. He still could make money in the ring. And he didn't think there was anyone around who could beat him, even then.

His manager, Marshall Miles, told Joe he thought it was time to retire, but his promoter, Mike Jacobs, told him he could make money with a fight or two. Jacobs arranged a 10-round exhibition bout for Joe with Jersey Joe Walcott in Madison Square Garden, but the New York State Athletic Commission said that if it was a 10-rounder it had to be for the heavyweight title. Rather than reduce it, Jacobs asked Joe to go 15 for the title and

Joe said that was all right with him. The press did not see Walcott as a fit foe for Louis, but the bout figured to draw well. A lot of people wanted to see Louis fight in what might be his last bout.

Walcott, born Arnold Cream in January of 1914 in New Jersey, was as old as Louis and a lot less accomplished. He had been boxing since 1930 and had lost 10 of 53 fights, three by knockouts. Tiger Jack Fox, Al Ettore, and Abe Simon had knocked him out. Louis, of course, had knocked out Ettore and Simon. Walcott, in fact, had lost two of his last five fights before fighting Louis. He dropped decisions to Joe Maxim and Elmer Ray before decisioning Ray once and Maxim twice in rematches. But Maxim was a clever boxer, who later would win the light-heavyweight title and "KO" Ray, a dangerous puncher.

Walcott was a lot like Jimmy Braddock in that he was unable to get a lot of fights and had to do a lot of hard work to support a large family through a considerable part of his career. For six years, from 1939 through 1944, for example, he had only seven fights. He was a lot like Jimmy Braddock in that he was not well trained or in shape for a lot of the bouts he lost, but he had a lot of natural ability and had developed a lot of ring savvy over the years. Jersey Joe had been one of Joe Louis's sparring partners prior to the first Max Schmeling fight, but had disappeared from camp after some rough sessions. Louis took him lightly, but Walcott was a bomb waiting to explode.

The Madison Square Garden match in December of 1947 drew 18,194 fans who paid $216,497 for the right to see what might be The Brown Bomber's last bout. The receipts surpassed the 20-year-old record Garden gate of $201,465 established by Jack Dempsey and Jim Maloney in 1927. But Louis was a 3–1 favorite and few expected Walcott to extend him.

Louis was slow at 211 pounds and Walcott, 17 pounds lighter at 194, was faster with his feet and hands. Flash right-hand punches to Joe's jaw floored Louis for a count of two in the second round and a count of seven in the fourth round and startled all in attendance. Louis was angry after the first one, but stunned by the second one and had to hold on as Walcott attacked to the bell.

Joe had been jabbing and looking for an opening for a big punch, while Jersey Joe had been dancing around, retreating, but it was Jersey Joe who spotted openings and jumped in with big punches. Suddenly, less than a third of the way through the fight, everyone knew it was a real fight and the champion was in real danger. Louis later recalled, "I'd see the openings, but before I could get my punch through them, they'd close. That's when I knew I'd lost something I'd never have again. My hands were slow. I couldn't pick off punches. My reflexes were slow. I'd see punches coming and couldn't duck in time. I knew I was in trouble. All that saved me is he wasn't daring enough. He was a careful fighter."

Cautiously, Walcott boxed Joe rather than punch with him. Walcott backpedaled while Louis chased him. Walcott was a funny fighter, a lot like Ali. He'd dance around, drop his hands, dare his foe to fire from long range, bob and weave, shuffle from side to side. His strange style confused the slowed-down Louis, who shuffled forward behind his still-jarring left jab, looking for openings for the left hook or right cross. Walcott didn't throw a lot of punches. He looked for other openings for the flash right, but when he saw them, he missed with his punches. He did cut Louis and damage his left eye.

Louis dominated the middle rounds of the fight, but until the ninth he couldn't catch Walcott with a hard blow. In the ninth he landed a right cross to the head, but it landed a little high. It shook Walcott and he had to cover up. Louis sailed into him with both fists, but the old finishing touch had faded. He missed as much as he landed. Walcott weathered the storm, and went back on his bicycle. Through the final third of the fight he kept dancing away, flicking at Louis with punches that taunted him while Louis shuffled forward in frustration, trying to catch his foe and failing.

With his two knockdown punches, Walcott thought he had won at the final bell. So did most of the crowd. Louis, his left eye swollen shut, thought he had lost. He started to duck out of the ring before the decision even was announced. Announcer Harry Balogh read the decision to the hushed listeners: "Referee Ruby Goldstein votes seven rounds for Walcott, six for Louis, and two even." A roar arose. "Judge Frank Forbes votes eight

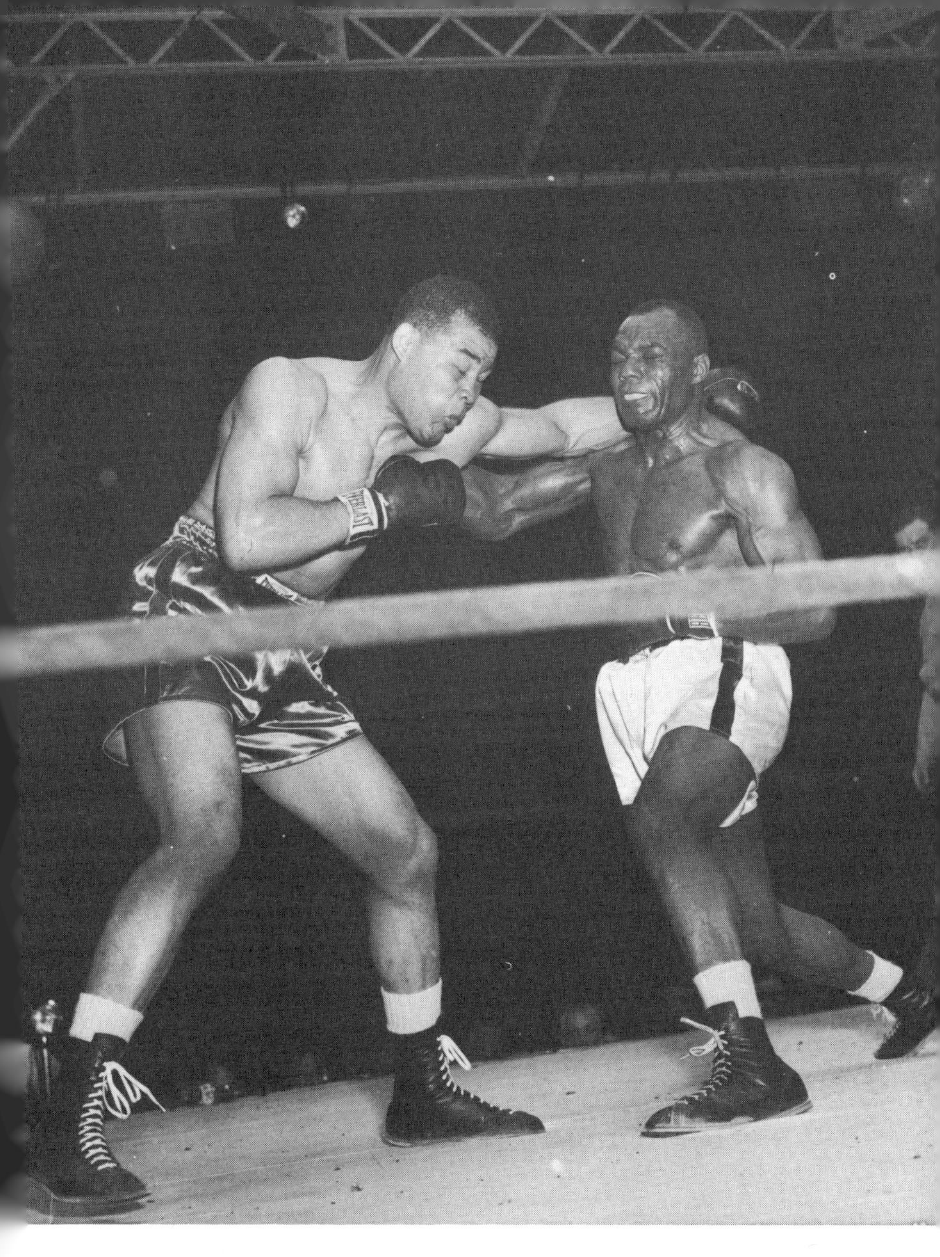

Jersey Joe Walcott digs a right to the body that makes Joe Louis wince as Joe missed with the left during rusty Bomber's close call at the Garden in December of 1947.

rounds for Louis, six for Walcott, and one even." Another roar, then a hush. "Judge Marty Monroe votes nine rounds to six for the winner—and still heavyweight champion of the world—Joe Louis." His last words were drowned out by the boos, which rained on the ring.

Humbled by the boos, Louis hurried from the ring. In his dressing room, head hung, he mumbled, "I thought I should win because he didn't come to me to take my title from me. But I'm sorry I put on such a bad fight. I don't know if I should fight again, but I think he deserves a return fight."

In his dressing room a disappointed Walcott said, "I hope he gives me another fight. I waited a long time for a chance and I thought I deserved the decision. No, I didn't punch with him. Who punches with Joe Louis? But I knocked him down twice. What do you have to do?" he asked mournfully, his voice drifting off. "I guess you have to knock him out to beat him," he said finally.

In the next morning's New York *Times*, James P. Dawson wrote, "Joe Louis is still the world heavyweight champion today because he won a split, unpopular decision over Jersey Joe Walcott, Camden, New Jersey, Negro challenger, last night. . . .

"By the same token, Walcott is not the heavyweight titleholder today because never in the history of the ring has a boxer won a championship running away without attempting a defensive counter-fire.

"Though he retained his title, Louis was nearer dethronement than he ever had been through his ten-year reign as the world's premier boxer. He was knocked down twice. . . . He was battered, bruised, and bleeding. He was outmaneuvered, at times outboxed . . . and generally made to look foolish.

"The Brown Bomber is past his peak. At thirty-three years of age, Louis is ripe for defeat. . . . The dread puncher whose very presence in the opposite corner often 'froze' a rival before hostilities began, definitely is on the downgrade. His reflexes are bad. His defense, never air-tight because it consisted chiefly of attack, is conspicuous by its absence."

Louis sat alone in a darkened room at his apartment for a long time after the fight, thinking about his future. He decided to go all out for one final fight, a rematch with Walcott, so he could go out in glory. He called his mother and she said she wanted him to give Walcott another chance, but that she wanted it to be his last fight.

He didn't go down to the Garden the next day, as he usually did, to pick up his check and joke with the press. The Garden got a lot of letters, telegrams, and telephone calls from people complaining that Walcott had deserved to win. Louis later said, "That was the first time the fans weren't with me."

Louis got his check, for a little more than $75,000. He figured to do better in the rematch, which was set for the following June in Yankee Stadium. Louis spent two months touring Europe, giving exhibition bouts in London, Paris, Brussels. He sailed on the *Queen Mary* with a large group and had a good time. But he was supposed to be guaranteed $80,000 and settled for half that as the promoter of the tour went bankrupt.

Louis trained hard for the rematch with Walcott, but went into the ring even heavier at 213 pounds. He was 34 years old now and it was not easy to get the weight off. Maybe because he was a lot hungrier, Walcott seemed a younger 34, a lot trimmer at 194. While Louis had trained for what he thought would be the last fight of his life, Walcott had trained for the biggest fight of his life. Louis still was favored at 3–2.

A crowd of more than 42,000 fans turned out on June 25, 1948, at the triple-tiered ballpark, and the scene was deep with drama. When Walcott knocked down Louis with a right to the cheekbone in the third round, it looked a lot like the first fight, it looked as if the Louis dynasty was over. The tension was terrific.

Far more confident than he had been before the first fight, Walcott boxed brilliantly and counterpunched effectively. Louis jumped right up from the knockdown, before the count even began, but that was the fastest he moved most of the night. He simply could not corner his dancing foe for most of the match and looked like a tired, beaten old man after ten rounds as the crowd booed the lack of action.

But in the 11th round Louis landed a right to the jaw that wobbled Walcott. Savagely Louis followed up with rights and lefts to the head. Hurt, Walcott retreated to the ropes, holding his hands high, trying to protect himself. Louis hammered away with both hands. A right hand burst through the defense and drilled Jersey Joe on the jaw. He fell, face first, onto the canvas and referee Frank Fullam commenced the count with the crowd roaring. At seven, Walcott rolled over on his back. He could not gather himself to get up. At ten, he was done.

In the next morning's New York *Times*, James P. Dawson paid a last tribute to the champ: "Because he has the punch that had made him one of the greatest heavyweights ever to hold the title, Joe Louis, the ring's Brown Bomber, still is the world champion. He knocked out Jersey Joe Walcott in the 11th round of an ordinary championship battle last night and plucked glorious, spectacular victory from threatened defeat.

"Trailing the challenger through ten rounds of fighting, which more than once drew jeers from the crowd, Louis turned the tide of battle with one punch. . . . Two of the officials had Walcott in front . . . Louis had to come off the floor to win this one, as he did last December. . . . Louis left the ring the conqueror, the champion, looking forward to retirement."

"I will retire," Louis admitted to reporters in his dressing room after the fight. "I wanted to go out the champ. He gave me a hard time and I'm happy to have won."

It was The Brown Bomber's 25th successful defense of the title he had held 11 years and a few days, and his 22nd knockout victory in that span. All were records. Only Tommy Farr, Arturo Godoy, and Joe Walcott had gone to a decision with him, and all had been knocked out in rematches. Louis had fought ten rematches with fighters and won them all by knockouts. He had avenged his only loss, to Max Schmeling, by one of his record ten first-round knockouts, a record five coming in title bouts. He had won 60 of 61 fights, 52 by knockout.

He had been knocked down eight times—once each by Jimmy Braddock, Buddy Baer, and Tony Galento, twice by Max Schmeling, and three times by Joe Walcott—but he had come back to knock out each one. He had been behind in the late stages of earlier bouts with Billy Conn and this one with Walcott, but he had dramatically knocked them out. He stood there in the ring at Yankee Stadium with the cheers sounding out of the dark night and he figured he was finished, finally.

He picked up a quarter-million dollars of the greater than $800,000 gate. That ran his earnings in title fights to better than two and a half million dollars. But he had little left and most of his latest paynight went to pay off debts. However, he could not go on forever and he wanted to go out as the champ, as only Gene Tunney had done before him. "I wanted to be known as the best," he admitted later.

He went back on the exhibition trail to pick up a thousand here, a thousand there, through the Deep South and across the country through the rest of 1948 and the first part of 1949 before formally announcing his retirement from the ring in March of 1949.

THE ROCKY COMEBACK

During Joe Louis's long reign as heavyweight champion, Mike Jacobs and the 20th Century Sporting Club promoted Madison Square Garden and New York ballpark bouts and dominated boxing across the country. Jacobs promoted not only Louis's heavyweight title matches, but most of those involving middleweight champions Tony Zale and Rocky Graziano, welterweight champion Sugar Ray Robinson, and featherweight champions Willie Pep and Sandy Saddler.

However, Jacobs had a stroke in December of 1946 and did not take an active part in Louis's last two title defenses in 1947 and 1948. Sol Strauss, Jacobs's cousin and associate, operated their promotional outfit. By the time Louis retired, Jacobs was seriously ill and inactive. When Harry Mendel, a press agent and a friend of Joe's, approached Louis with a way to continue to make money in boxing, Louis listened.

Jim Norris, who owned the Chicago Stadium and a piece of Madison Square Garden, as well as hockey's Chicago Black Hawks and Detroit Red Wings, was a wealthy sportsman who was interested in taking over Garden and New York boxing promotions from Mike Jacobs just as Jacobs had wanted to take these from Jimmy Johnston years earlier when Louis first entered the picture.

Mendel put Louis in touch with Norris. Louis brought Truman Gibson into the picture to deal for him. The deal that was developed with Norris and an associate, Arthur Wirtz, was that Louis would become a vice president in a newly formed International Boxing Club and would receive a $300,000 bonus and a salary of $30,000 a year to front for the outfit and promote title matches. Gibson became an officer in the outfit and Mendel got a piece of the action.

With the approval of Abe Greene, president of the National Boxing Association, which ruled, rather loosely, the ring sport in this country, the IBC, through Louis, named Joe Walcott and Ezzard Charles to fight for the vacated heavyweight title in June of 1949 at the Chicago Stadium. Charles won a 15-round decision to win general recognition as champion.

Charles successfully defended his crown by knocking out Gus Lesnevich in New York in August, Pat Valentino in San Francisco in October, and Freddy Beshore in Buffalo in August of the following year, 1950. Most of the knockouts Charles scored were because he'd cut his opponent so badly the referee stopped the fight. He was a skilled boxer who punished opponents, but he was not a heavy hitter or strong gate attraction.

New York was one state which did not recognize Charles as champion, and Norris decided that Louis should fight Charles for the title so the winner would receive recognition everywhere. He wanted Louis to lose his title in the ring so his successor could be promoted to prominence.

Louis was playing promoter, but he did not even attend all of Charles's title fights. He was getting by on his IBC money, but remained deep in debt. He had remained active in exhibition bouts and believed he could beat Charles, who really was not much more than a light-heavyweight. He agreed to meet Charles in September of 1950 at Yankee Stadium.

Louis underrated Charles. Everyone did. He may have been the most underrated of fighters. Born in July of 1921 in Georgia but reared in Ohio, Charles won all 44 of his amateur bouts and ten AAU, Diamond Belt, and Golden Gloves tournament titles. He won his first 20 pro bouts before being beaten by middleweight champion Ken Overlin and drew with Overlin in a rematch. Before he went into service during World War II, Charles also lost to Kid Tunero, Jimmy Bivins, and Lloyd Marshall. Bivins won recognition as "interim heavyweight champion" while Louis was in service.

In service, Charles had an undefeated career in Army tournaments. Discharged from service, he twice decisioned Bivins and knocked out Marshall. He lost to Elmer Ray, but knocked him out in a rematch. He decisioned Joey Maxim five times, decisioned Archie Moore twice and knocked him out once, and knocked out Anton Christoforidis, and all three won the light-heavyweight title. At the time he met Louis for the title, Charles had won 19 straight fights, had lost only one of 35 since leaving the service, and had lost only four of 66 fights since turning pro in 1939. He was just 29 years old and at his peak as a skilled, stylish performer.

Louis had not fought for two years and three months and was 36 years old when he went into the ring with Charles. He was soft at 218 pounds, while Charles was hard at 184 pounds. Louis was a 2–1 favorite, but that was foolishness. It didn't figure to be much of a fight and it wasn't. Only 13,562 fans showed up and they saw Charles, though boxing cautiously, slice Louis's face wide open and dominate the bout from beginning to end, winning 10, 12, and 13 rounds on the official scorecards. Slow and clumsy, Louis tried desperately, but was unable to land a single punch of consequence.

James P. Dawson's New York *Times* story read: "A great champion went into the discard last night at the Yankee Stadium, the fightingest world heavyweight champion boxing ever knew, as Ezzard Charles pounded Joe Louis into a bleeding, helpless hulk to become the undisputed holder of the heavyweight crown. . . .

"Charles won the recognition through 15 rounds of bruising fighting, in which he hammered Louis as he pleased, punched Joe around the ring as if he were an inanimate punching bag, outboxed, outfought, outmaneuvered what was once a great champion in a manner that proved, once again, the truth of the ring legend, 'they never come back.' "

Louis said later, "Even before the fight, sitting in my dressing room, I wanted to tell Manny Seamon to call it off, but I knew I couldn't. I knew in training I didn't have it. When I got into the fight, I saw early I didn't have it. I thought my weight advantage might help, but it didn't. All I had was a jab. Halfway through the fight, I was so tired I didn't think I could continue. By the end of the fight they practically had to lift me off my stool to get me going. I was just glad when it was over."

He was cheered as he left the ring, but only for old times' sake. He was embarrassed by it. He was embarrassed as he sat, bruised and bloody, in his dressing room and apologized to the press for his performance. He said, "I wasn't any good, but Charles was very good. Give him the credit. I guess I fought one time too many. I'll get out for good now."

But the $50,000 he received from the mere $200,000 gate did little to ease his financial problems. And the more he thought about it, the more he thought he could defeat Charles if he really went back to work and got back in good shape. He was just one of many athletes who can't accept the toll the years take, who can't accept the fact that the ability they once had is gone forever, who can't bring themselves to give up when it's time to give up.

"You go on and the years slip by and you hardly notice," Louis said later. "Outside the ring, you don't feel that much older. You were the best and you can't believe you can't still be the best. You like bein' champ. You don't want to stop. You kid yourself."

Norris figured he could still make some money with Louis and wanted him to go on. Louis figured he could erase the embarrassment of the Charles fight. So he announced he was continuing his comeback and returned to training. He worked hard, and it was hard work for him, now. He got to be about as good as he could be at that point in his career. He had the left jab, which was still lethal. He had punching power, when he could land a good punch.

Late in November, two months after the Charles loss, Louis decisioned an Argentinian, Cesar Brion, over 10 rounds at Chicago Stadium. In January of 1951, he knocked out Freddie Beshore in four rounds in Detroit. In February, he decisioned Omelio Agramonte in 10 in Miami and knocked out Andy Walker in 10 in San Francisco. In May, he decisioned Agramonte in 10 again in Detroit. In mid-June, he returned to New York and knocked out Lee Savold in six rounds in the Garden. Savold was a ranking contender and Louis looked fairly good. Some thought he was on his way back to the title.

Following the Louis bout, Charles successfully defended his title by knocking out Nick Barone and Lee Oma and decisioning Joe Walcott twice, making it three in a row over Jersey Joe. However, each one was close. After decisioning Joey Maxim in May of 1951, Charles gave Walcott yet another title shot and ran into an uppercut which flattened him in the seventh round. Louis figured, well, if not Charles, I'll just have to whip Walcott again to get back the title.

In August, Louis decisioned Cesar Brion in 10 again in San Francisco and decisioned Jimmy Bivins, "the interim champ," in 10 in Baltimore. He now had won eight straight in the second stage of his comeback and while only three had come by KO, many figured Louis still was the best in the business. But a third fight with Walcott didn't look like a big-money heavyweight title match to Norris, who suggested that Louis take on Rocky Marciano first. Rocky was a red-hot comer and Norris coldly calculated that either Marciano would establish himself as a big gate attraction by beating the ex-champ or Louis would re-establish himself as a draw by beating the hot kid.

Rocky was no kid at 28, but he'd started late as a boxer and was just approaching his peak. Born in September of 1923 in Brockton, Massachusetts, the "Brockton Blockbuster" was a brawling fighter, short in height and short-armed, short on science, but rock-hard and heavy-handed. He had won 37 straight fights, 32 by knockouts. But he was awkward, wide open, and unpolished. Louis, who would have a big edge in height, reach, and weight, figured that with his left jab he could outbox his inexperienced foe and maybe nail him with a big punch.

The match was made for October 26, 1951, in Madison Square Garden. Louis went to Pompton Lakes and trained hard and well. The big writers, name athletes, movie and television stars came to watch him and flatter him. It was just like the good old days and Louis started to feel like a champ again. He trained down below 213 pounds, but he looked like a large, old Louis. His hair was thinning out, his face was round, his stomach soft. He was made an 8–5 favorite and he felt confident going in, but he later admitted, "I was kidding myself. I was confident, but I was kidding myself."

There were 17,241 paying customers in the grand old Garden that night and great excitement everywhere. The outer lights went out and the large ex-champ and stocky challenger moved out under the spotlights. Within a few minutes, Louis was staggered with a long, looping right hand he was too slow to duck. That was the way it was going to be and everyone could see it early. Louis left-jabbed Marciano into a bloody mess, but Joe was too slow to catch him with a power punch and too slow to avoid all Marciano's long, looping blows.

By the eighth round of the scheduled 10-rounder, Louis was weary. "My legs were so tired I could hardly stand up," he admitted later. It is said that if he could have lasted he could have won, but it is not true. It is said he was ahead, but the fact is the official scorecards had him losing on rounds, 4–3, 4–2–1, and 5–2. And he was fading fast.

Early in the eighth, Louis drove a wicked right to the ribs, but Rocky kept coming. Louis was trying to reach Rocky with rights to the head, but Marciano stepped inside the blows and hooked with the left. He forced Joe to the ropes and landed a left hook to the jaw that sent Joe to the canvas.

The fans were screaming as Louis struggled up at the count of seven. Marciano flew wildly at him, throwing rights and lefts. Most missed, but two left hooks hammered Louis's head and left him standing, dazed, his arms at his sides. Marciano saw that Joe was helpless and launched a thundering right which crashed against the ex-champ's chin. Louis went through the ring ropes, landing on the apron of the ring. It was the tenth time he had been knocked down in his career—and the last.

He was finished. Everyone could see it. Referee Ruby Goldstein waved his hands, signaling that the fight was stopped. The fans stood. Some cheered Rocky. Others wept for The Brown Bomber. Dr. Vincent Nardiello, the ringside physician and an old friend, cradled the ex-champ's head in his lap. Sugar Ray Robinson, by now world middleweight champion and an old friend from the early days in Detroit, had come out of his seat to crouch by Joe's side, and he wept. It was as though a king had died.

The next day's *Times* story, written by Joseph C. Nichols, read:

"Joe Louis was knocked out last night.

"The once incomparable Brown Bomber of the dreaded punch and electric reflexes lost to Rocky Marciano, undefeated battler from Brockton, Mass., in the

Rocky Marciano turns his back and walks away from a fallen, 37-year-old Joe Louis as a classic career comes to an end at Madison Square Garden in October of 1951.

eighth round of a scheduled ten-round bout at Madison Square Garden.

"At least, the record books will say that it was Marciano who beat Joe, but everybody knows it was age. The years were against the 37-year-old Louis as he plodded through seven dreary rounds with his rival, ten years younger."

Joe Louis's career had come to an end. The retirement he announced after that fight was for real. He lay on his dressing-room table, an ice bag pressed to his swollen face, and said graciously, "The better man won," but after most of the reporters had left he sighed and said sadly, "The years beat me, not Rocky. He's good, but I was the best."

Maybe. If you count the Charles fight as the real end of his reign, he ruled the heavyweights for 13 years and three months. He fought 18 years as a professional and won 68 of 71 bouts, 55 by knockouts. He was decisioned only once and lost twice by knockouts. Two of his three defeats came after his original retirement. He never lost a rematch and had a dozen. He met the best in boxing in his day and defended his title far more times than any other fighter.

Walcott kept his title on a controversial decision in a rematch with Charles in June of 1952, but lost it on a knockout to Marciano in September of 1952. The fight was amazingly like the first Louis–Conn contest with the boxer outpointing the puncher and on the verge of scoring an upset when the puncher pulled it out with a 13th-round knockout.

Marciano held the title only three years and successfully defended it six times, including two tough triumphs over Ezzard Charles, before retiring after knocking out Archie Moore in September of 1956. Rocky did not come back and so became the only undefeated heavyweight champion. His record of 49–0 included 43 KO's and since he never lost, it is possible he never would have lost. He has to be considered one of the greatest, if not the greatest, of the heavyweight champions.

Floyd Patterson knocked out Archie Moore in November of 1956 to fill the vacant title, lost it to Ingemar Johansson on a knockout in June of 1960, regained it on a knockout of Johannsson in June of 1959, becoming the first man to regain the crown, then lost it, finally, on a knockout to Sonny Liston in September of 1962.

Liston lost it on a knockout to Cassius Clay in February of 1964. Clay adopted the name Muhammad Ali and reigned until refusing to enter service when drafted during the Vietnamese conflict in the late 1960s. After Ali was stripped of his title, Joe Frazier won recognition as champion by knocking out Jimmy Ellis in February of 1970. Some considered Ali king until he came back and was outpointed by Frazier in a title match in March of 1971.

Frazier lost the crown when knocked out by George Foreman in January of 1973. Ali regained the laurel by knocking out Foreman in October of 1974. He lost it to

Leon Spinks on a decision in February of 1978, the first time the title had changed hands on a decision since Braddock beat Baer in 1935, more than 40 years earlier, but regained it from Spinks on a decision in September of that year before retiring with the title. With 56 victories in 59 professional bouts, 37 knockout victories and no knockout defeats, and with 20 defenses during the almost ten years he held the title over three reigns, Ali stands as the second most enduring and active heavyweight champion and one of the greatest.

Jim Jeffries, Jack Johnson, and Jack Dempsey have to be ranked, along with Rocky Marciano, among the best, too, though they did not defend the title as Louis did or as Ali later did. It is difficult to judge Jeffries or Johnson, though films of their fights do not make them look as good as later fighters. And Ali came along in a recent time when boxing was not as big, nor were there as many good fighters to fight as earlier.

Ali has been a great boxer, not a great puncher, and his greatest asset may have been his ability to take a punch. It is possible he would have been too fast for Louis, been able to take his best shots and outpointed him, but Billy Conn couldn't do it and it may be more possible that Louis would have nailed Ali. Ali had terrible trouble with brawlers like Joe Frazier and Ken Norton. Neither Frazier nor Norton is a Jack Dempsey or Rocky Marciano, who presumably then might have overpowered Ali. They could hit and Louis could be hit, so they might have taken him out. But they were wide open and it might be more likely that Louis's fast hands and powerful punches would have taken them out.

The best in a sport seldom develop at the same time, so one can only imagine bouts between these heavy-weight champions at their peaks. Those who lived through the Joe Louis era believe The Brown Bomber was the best ever, and when his spectacular era came to an end in the fall of 1951 it was a sad moment in the history of sports.

RETIREMENT

Even in retirement, Joe Louis remained "the champ" to most people. His image was so good that even the brilliance of Rocky Marciano could not take the spotlight away from The Brown Bomber. It was not until many years had passed and Muhammad Ali stole the spotlight that Louis was overshadowed. Even then, 25 years or so after retirement, Joe was recognized wherever he went and received standing ovations when he attended a big fight or other sporting event.

It was not that he had done so much for the blacks, although he gave them great pride in their race and opened doors for Jackie Robinson and others to pass through, but that he had been a great athlete who performed gallantly and did honor to boxing and to all sports. As sportswriter Jimmy Cannon wrote, "He is a credit to his race—the human race."

He did not, of course, live a blameless life outside the ring, but if he was imperfect, which of us isn't? He wanted to have a good time, he had a weakness for women, and money meant nothing to him. But, outside the ring, he never deliberately hurt anyone and he made a great many friends and practically no enemies, not even among his ex-wives.

After Marva divorced him for the second and last time, she married Dr. Albert Spaulding in 1950. She took Jackie and Joe, Jr., but Joe used to take them often, and not only them, but also a daughter, Alvita, Marva had with Dr. Spaulding, and they all called him "Daddy Joe." He hadn't been around for the birth of either of his children and he never spent a lot of time with either of them, but he did care for them, and he gave them whatever they wanted.

On Christmas day, 1955, he married Rose Morgan, a black businesswoman who developed and distributed beauty products for black women. But his style of life hadn't changed. He was still attractive to the ladies and he still wasn't home much. She finally gave up and they separated in 1957 and received an annulment of their marriage, which meant it had never really been a marriage, in 1958.

In 1960, Joe married Martha Malone Jefferson, a black lawyer, and moved into her sprawling, Spanish-style, 10-room house in the Crenshaw area of Los Angeles. He saw to it that there was a television set in every room, even the bathroom, and he liked to lie around all day watching game shows. He had even gone on a game show, "High Finance" with Dennis James, lasting six weeks and winning $25,000.

Joe also liked to golf in the mornings and go out nights.

At 44, the retired Brown Bomber has just taken his third and last wife, Martha Jefferson, a 46-year-old lawyer, at Winterhaven, California, in March of 1959.

One of his girl friends had a baby boy she said was Joe's. Joe said it was probably his, so Martha suggested they adopt it, which they did, naming it Joseph, although he already had a Joe, Jr. Martha was a very understanding woman. She didn't even mind when Joe called her "Marva" by mistake. When the same lady had a baby boy and two baby girls later, which probably weren't Joe's, Joe and Martha adopted them too, naming them John and Joyce and Janet. The lady just kept having babies and Joe and Martha just kept adopting them. Soon their house was full of kids.

Martha was a marvelous mother and wife. She took Joe for what he was. She said, "If I take a man, I treat him right." She accepted it when Joe was gone and treated him like a king when he was home. He still was gone a lot, but now he looked forward to going home. One of his girl friends turned him onto drugs, but Martha helped him kick the habit. His mind deteriorated, as his dad's had before him, and he was in and out of hospitals, but Martha nursed him back to health each time.

He lay in his bed in their house in L.A. one night when he was 50 and he said, "I got me a good wife. Had all good wives. Loved 'em all. And they love each other. Rose even gives Martha beauty treatments, you know that? And Marva and Martha get together and gossip 'bout me. Got lots to gossip about," he chuckled. "Ladies added a lot to my life. Loved 'em all. Added a lot of kids. Nice kids. Loved 'em all."

He was watching television and he kept changing channels with a remote control unit as he talked. At 240 pounds, he was about 40 pounds above his best fighting weight and he looked a little fat, but he looked fine. He spoke slowly and didn't have a lot to say, but he always spoke slowly and he never had a lot to say. He seemed alert and, as always, what he said made sense.

"I wouldn't change anything in my life if I had it to do over again. I made the most of my ability and I did my best with my title. I don't even regret coming back and losing my title and losing a few fights. A title should be won and lost in the ring, and it's no disgrace to get old and to lose. I didn't disgrace myself by fighting a few more years. I liked fighting and won a few more fights. My record's all right.

"The money don't matter. I guess the five million I made in my day would have been fifty million today, but if I made fifty million I'd have spent it just like I spent the five million. I'd have gambled it away or given it away. I'm sorry I didn't pay everyone I owed, but I paid as many people as much as I could. I miss the people more than they missed the money," he said.

When Mike Jacobs, John Roxborough, and Julian Black died, Louis was in debt to them. But Jacobs left an estate of six million dollars, while Roxborough and Black were well fixed financially to the end. Louis earned close to four million dollars in his professional fights and more than a million more in exhibition bouts, but he wound up with nothing.

With interest and penalties, Joe owed $1,300,000 in taxes before the government agreed to give up on it. Celebrities staged benefit shows on his behalf and at one point he agreed to pay $20,000 a year, but he couldn't keep it up. After a while, officials simply stopped pursuing it. It was unpopular with the public, which loved Louis.

He had blown another $100,000 in another restaurant that folded in Harlem. He blew money in a beer business he went into and he didn't make much on soft drinks and milk marketed in his name. He had an advertising agency with Billy Rowe that made him money, but he was criticized for representing Fidel Castro and Cuba and for a friendship with teamsters' union boss Jimmy Hoffa.

After retiring in October of 1951, Joe boxed exhibitions in the Far East, mainly with servicemen, during the Korean war, until almost the end of the year. His last exhibition bout was on December 16, 1951, at Taipei, Formosa. *The Joe Louis Story* was made into a movie starring Golden Gloves champ Coley Wallace, a heavyweight who looked a little like Joe, but it wasn't much of a movie and Wallace wasn't much of a fighter after he turned pro.

Joe's mother died in 1953 and that depressed him deeply. The government took trust funds he had set up for his kids to pay off back taxes, so when Joe was offered $100,000 in 1956 to go on tour wrestling, he took it. It was, in a way, the low point of his life. Professional wrestling is not for real, but Joe didn't mind. He put on the best show he could until a 340-pounder, Cowboy Rocky Lee, landed on Joe's chest, fractured his ribs, and did some damage to his heart. As one Rocky had ended Joe's boxing career, another ended his wrestling career.

So long as Jim Norris and the IBC were in business, Joe was in for $30,000 a year. And the IBC dominated boxing as Mike Jacobs' 20th Century Sporting Club never had. Jacobs had started televising boxing matches with the Max Baer–Lou Nova bout back in 1941 and started weekly telecasts in 1944. But when Norris took over after World War II, he took the ball and ran with it with Friday night fights from the Garden and Wednesday night fights from Chicago Stadium and elsewhere.

Rivals promoted televised matches other nights of the week as boxing hit its video heyday, but Gillette Razor Blade's "Cavalcade of Sports" show on Friday nights from the Garden were the big bouts and brought the IBC about $15 million over 15 years before they ended in 1964, when the government broke up what it considered an IBC monopoly on the ring game.

Rocky Marciano's title fights went on closed circuit into theaters, but Sugar Ray Robinson, Carmen Basilio, Gene Fullmer, Archie Moore, Joey Maxim, Kid Gavilan, Johnny Saxton, Jimmy Carter, Tiger Jones, Willie Pep, Sandy Saddler, and many more became big stars on the home screen. Boxing suffered as clubs closed all across the country when the fans stayed home to watch the best in the business in their living rooms.

Louis refereed boxing and wrestling matches for a while and tried promoting fights, first at the Sports Arena, then at the Moulin Rouge night club in L.A. in the 1960s. He even had a local TV contract for a while, but he couldn't get the extraordinary fighters to fight for him and he paid extraordinary money for ordinary fighters. He failed.

He sat in a corner of the club sipping a soft drink one night, and he said, "The problem with boxing today is nobody wants to fight anybody any good. In my day, you fought the guy who was ahead of you in the ratings so you could get ahead. If you were champ, you fought the number one contender, then the number two contender. You were a fighter, so you fought."

He sighed and said, "I always thought promoters made too much and fighters too little, so I tried to pay my fighters more as a promoter, but these fighters want to fight nobodies for big bucks. I guess I was cut out to be a fighter. I was never cut out to be a promoter like Mike Jacobs."

He was asked if Mike or his managers took too much from him. In his honest way, he said, "No. We made money for each other. They gave me money whenever I wanted it. I owed them money when they died, so how can they have cheated me? Don't blame them. Blame me. Don't blame anyone. It just happened. It was just money. It just wasn't important."

Martha straightened out Joe's tangled financial affairs so he could continue to get around in comfort. He acted as host at night clubs in London and Las Vegas before Caesar's Palace in Vegas made him a host, gave him and his family a house in which Frank Sinatra used to live, and put him on salary.

All Joe had to do was hang around the hotel and casino, greet customers, sign autographs, make small talk with his fans, once in a while take a trip on behalf of Caesar's. And that's what he did in the 1970s. And he liked it. He liked it that he was still called "champ." He liked talking about fights.

"Billy Conn was the best I ever fought," he said one night in the coffee shop at Caesar's. "Ezzard Charles, Joe Walcott, and Rocky Marciano were among the best. I beat Billy when I was at my best and I beat Joe even after I was at my best. I didn't have much left when I lost to Charles and Marciano, but they still didn't make me look too bad. At my best, I think I could've beaten them.

"Ali? He's been good, but I don't think he's been the best. Conn or Charles or even Jersey Joe could've boxed with him and Marciano or me would have outpunched him. I didn't box bad, you know. Only lost one decision. I got knocked down, but I got up. Ali made too many mistakes to last with me. But that's just the way I see it. We all see us as the best. Ali says he's the greatest, let him say it. Don't cost me nothing," Joe laughed.

He left to play another round of golf. He played with Bob Hope and Bing Crosby, Sammy Davis and Redd Foxx. He played with the big names, but he was always

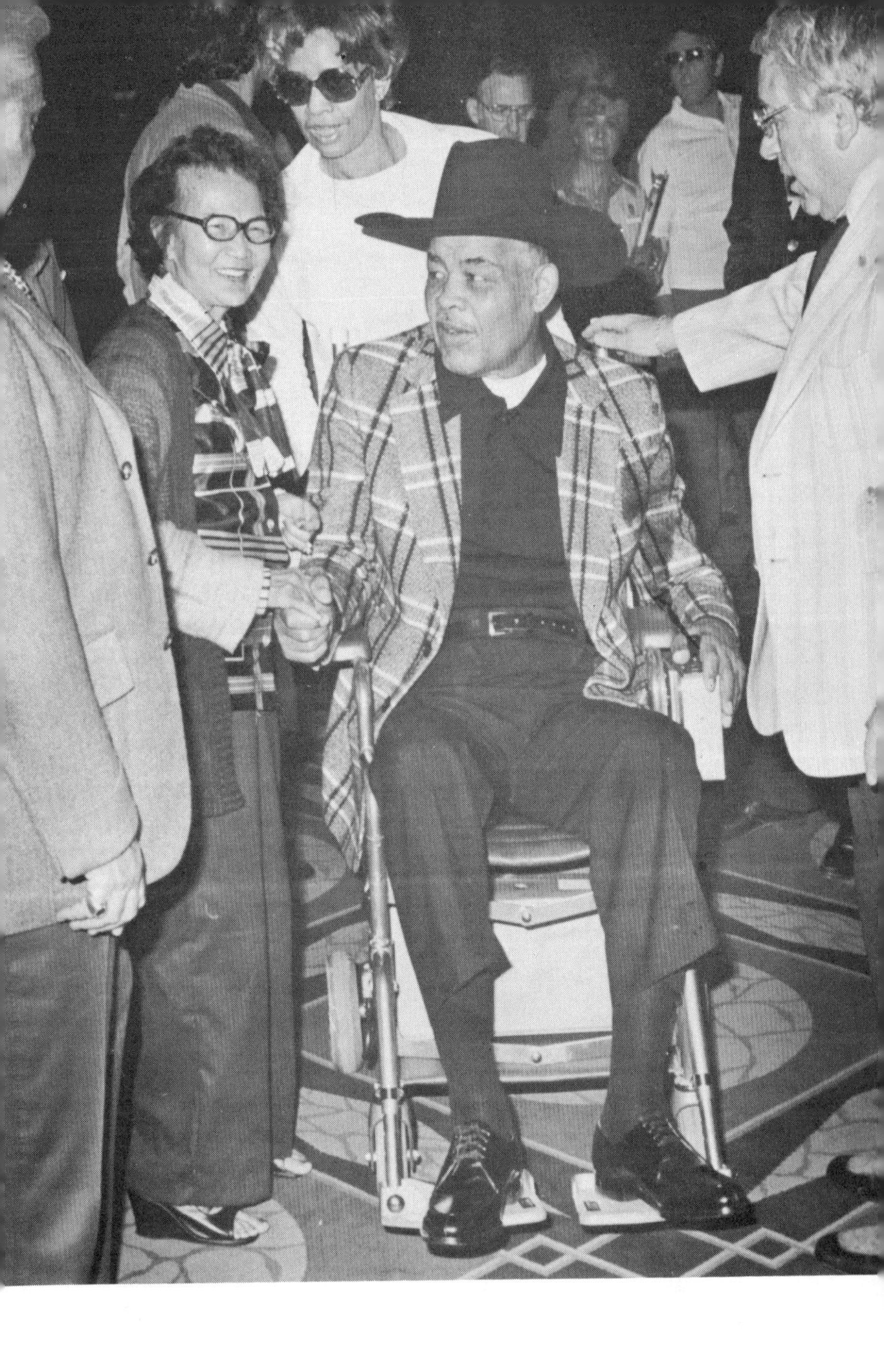

the biggest name in any game. He didn't give up the game until he suffered a stroke, which left him with limited speech and movement.

In May of 1979 they gave him a party for his sixty-fifth birthday. Every year they gave him a party on his birthday. The year before they had given him a big party at Caesar's, and Frank Sinatra, who had picked up the tab when Joe needed surgery, emceed the affair, which was attended by Cary Grant, Gregory Peck, Barbra Streisand, Dean Martin, Milton Berle, Telly Savalas, Clint Eastwood, and other show business stars.

Billy Conn, Tony Galento, and others Louis had knocked out came. Even Max Schmeling. They'd come other times, too, to honor Joe. And Muhammad Ali, who waved at Louis, sitting in his wheelchair, and said with unusual modesty, "There is the man who really deserves to be called 'the greatest.'" Everyone stood and cheered Joe, who managed a grateful smile.

Then they showed a film of Joe in the 13th round with Conn. And there he was once again—young, hard, deadly, shuffling forward behind that lethal left hook, pumping it in his foe's face, hooking with the left suddenly, firing the right so fast the eye couldn't follow it, rallying gallantly, exploding dynamite, coming from behind to finish off a foe with a graceful, swift fury that can never be forgotten.

HISTORY OF THE HEAVYWEIGHT TITLE

Date	*New Champion*	*Loser*	*How*	*Held Title*	*Defens*
Feb. 7, 1882	John L. Sullivan	Paddy Ryan	KO 9	10 Yrs. 7 Mos.	3 *
Sept. 7, 1892	James J. Corbett	Sullivan	KO 21	4 Yrs. 6 Mos.	2 *
March 17, 1897	Bob Fitzsimmons	Corbett	KO 14	2 Yrs. 3 Mos.	1
June 9, 1899	James J. Jeffries	Fitzsimmons	KO 11	5 Yrs. 2 Mos.	5 **
July 3, 1905	Marvin Hart	Jack Root	KO 12	7 Mos.	1
Feb. 23, 1906	Tommy Burns	Hart	W 20	2 Yrs. 10 Mos.	12
Dec. 26, 1908	Jack Johnson	Burns	KO 14	6 Yrs. 4 Mos.	8
April 5, 1915	Jess Willard	Johnson	KO 26	4 Yrs. 2 Mos.	2
July 4, 1919	Jack Dempsey	Willard	KO 3	7 Yrs. 2 Mos.	6
Sept. 23, 1926	Gene Tunney	Dempsey	W 10	1 Yr. 10 Mos.	2 ***
June 12, 1930	Max Schmeling	Jack Sharkey	Fl. 4	3 Yrs. 9 Mos.	2
June 21, 1932	Jack Sharkey	Schmeling	W 15	1 Yr.	1
June 29, 1933	Primo Carnera	Sharkey	KO 6	1 Yr.	3
June 14, 1934	Max Baer	Carnera	KO 11	1 Yr.	1
June 13, 1935	James Braddock	Baer	W 15	2 Yrs.	1
June 22, 1937	Joe Louis	Braddock	KO 8	11 Yrs.	25 **
June 22, 1949	Ezzard Charles	Joe Walcott	W 15	2 Yrs. 1 Mo.	9
July 18, 1951	Joe Walcott	Charles	KO 7	13 Mos.	2
Sept. 23, 1952	Rocky Marciano	Walcott	KO 13	4 Yrs.	6 ***
Nov. 30, 1956	Floyd Patterson	Archie Moore	KO 5	2 Yrs. 7 Mos.	5
June 26, 1959	Ingemar Johansson	Patterson	KO 3	1 Yr.	1
June 20, 1960	Patterson	Johansson	KO 5	1 Yr. 3 Mos.	3
Sept. 25, 1962	Sonny Liston	Patterson	KO 1	1 Yr. 5 Mos.	2
Feb. 25, 1964	Cassius Clay (Muhammad Ali)	Liston	KO 7	6 Yrs.	9
Feb. 16, 1970	Joe Frazier	Jimmy Ellis	KO 5	2 Yrs. 11 Mos.	5
Jan. 22, 1973	George Foreman	Frazier	KO 2	1 Yr. 9 Mos.	3
Oct. 30, 1974	Muhammad Ali	Foreman	KO 8	3 Yrs. 3 Mos.	11
Feb. 15, 1978	Leon Spinks	Ali	W 15	9 Mos.	1
Sept., 1978	Muhammad Ali****	Spinks	W 15	0	0 ***

* Sullivan, the first to gain international recognition as champion, fought more than 20 times after taking title, but most were for few rounds

and only a 39-round draw with Charley Mitchell and a 75-round knockout of Jake Kilrain, the last "bare-knuckles" bout, were regarded as title fights prior to the Corbett bout.

Corbett had only a 3-round KO of Charley Mitchell regarded as a title defense prior to the Fitzsimmons bout.

** Jeffries's last fight as champion before retirement was in August, 1904, but he was regarded as champion by many until Burns took vacant title and by others until defeated by Jack Johnson in July, 1910.

Louis's last fight as champion before retirement was June, 1948, but he was regarded as champion by many until Charles took vacant title and by others until defeated by Charles in September, 1950.

*** Tunney and Marciano retired with title and did not come back. Tunney's last fight was July, 1928, and Marciano's April, 1963.

Ali's last fight as champ was September of 1978, though he did not announce retirement until June of 1979. Earlier, he was stripped of his title in March of 1967, but was regarded as champion by many until Frazier won vacated title in February, 1970, and by others until he lost to Frazier in March, 1971.

**** After Ali retired, Larry Holmes gained recognition as champion by the World Boxing Council and John Tate gained recognition as champion by the World Boxing Association. Tate then lost his share of the title to Mike Weaver early in 1980. Weaver and Holmes thus shared the disputed title when Ali indicated in 1980 that he might try to win back the title.

JOE LOUIS'S RING RECORD

Date	*Foe*	*Result*	*City*	*Earnings*
		1934		
July 4	Jack Kracken	KO 1	Chicago	$ 52
July 11	Willie Davis	KO 3	Chicago	60
July 29	Larry Udell	KO 2	Chicago	106
Aug. 13	Jack Kranz	W 6	Chicago	125
Aug. 27	Buck Everett	KO 2	Chicago	150
Sept. 11	Alex Borchuk	KO 4	Detroit	106
Sept. 24	Adolph Wiater	W 10	Chicago	200
Oct. 24	Art Sykes	KO 8	Chicago	280
Oct. 30	Jack O'Dowd	KO 2	Detroit	111
Nov. 14	Stanley Poreda	KO 1	Chicago	300
Nov. 30	Charles Massera	KO 3	Chicago	1,100
Dec. 14	Lee Ramage	KO 8	Chicago	2,500

Year: 12(10)-0 Year: $5,090

Date	*Foe*	*Result*	*City*	*Earnings*
		1935		
Jan. 4	Patsy Perroni	W 10	Detroit	4,200
Jan. 11	Hans Birkie	KO 10	Pittsburgh	1,900
Feb. 21	Lee Ramage	KO 2	Los Angeles	4,354
March 8	Don (Red) Barry	KO 3	San Francisco	3,270
March 28	Natie Brown	W 10	Detroit	6,589
April 12	Roy Lazer	KO 3	Chicago	11,212
April 22	Biff Benton	KO 2	Dayton	750
April 27	Roscoe Toles	KO 6	Flint, Mich.	1,250
May 3	Willie Davis	KO 2	Peoria, Ill.	750
May 7	Gene Stanton	KO 3	Kalamazoo, Mich.	750
June 25	Primo Carnera	KO 6	New York City	60,433
Aug. 7	King Levinsky	KO 1	Chicago	53,752
Sept. 24	Max Baer	KO 4	New York City	240,833
Dec. 13	Paolino Uzcudun	KO 4	New York City	39,612

Year: 14(12)-0 Career: 26(22)-0 Year: $429,655

Date	*Foe*	*Result*	*City*	*Earnings*
		1936		
Jan. 17	Charley Retzlaff	KO 1	Chicago	23,065
June 19	Max Schmeling	*KO'd 12*	New York City	125,535
Aug. 17	Jack Sharkey	KO 3	New York City	36,506
Sept. 22	Al Ettore	KO 5	Philadelphia	52,897
Oct. 9	Jorge Brescia	KO 3	New York City	8,411
Dec. 14	Eddie Simms	KO 1	Cleveland	20,000

Year: 5(5)-1(1) Career: 31(27)-1(1) Year: $266,414

Date	*Foe*	*Result*	*City*	*Earnings*
		1937		
Jan. 11	Steve Ketchell	KO 2	Buffalo	3,100
Jan. 29	Bob Pastor	W 10	New York City	36,000
Feb. 17	Natie Brown	KO 4	Kansas City	11,000
June 22	* James J. Braddock (Won title)	KO 8	Chicago	103,084
Aug. 30	* Tommy Farr	W 15	New York City	102,578

Year: 5(3)-0 Career: 36(30)-1(1) Year: $255,762

Date	*Foe*	*Result*	*City*	*Earnings*
		1938		
Feb. 22	* Nathan Mann	KO 3	New York City	40,522
April 1	* Harry Thomas	KO 5	Chicago	16,659
June 22	* Max Schmeling	KO 1	New York City	349,228

Year: 3(3)-0 Career: 39(33)-1(1) Year: $406,409

Date	*Foe*	*Result*	*City*	*Earnings*
		1939		
Jan. 25	* John Henry Lewis	KO 1	New York City	34,413
April 17	* Jack Roper	KO 1	Los Angeles	34,850
June 28	* Tony Galento	KO 4	New York City	114,332
Sept. 20	* Bob Pastor	KO 11	Detroit	118,400

Year: 4(4)-0 Career: 43(37)-1(1) Year: $301,995

Date	*Foe*	*Result*	*City*	*Earnings*
		1940		
Feb. 9	* Arturo Godoy	W 15	New York City	23,620
March 29	* John Paychek	KO 2	New York City	19,908
June 20	* Arturo Godoy	KO 8	New York City	55,989
Dec. 16	* Al McCoy	KO 6	Boston	17,938
	Year: 4(3)-0 Career: 47(40)-1(1) Year: $117,455			
		1941		
Jan. 31	* Red Burman	KO 5	New York City	21,023
Feb. 17	* Gus Dorazio	KO 2	Philadelphia	18,730
March 21	* Abe Simon	KO 13	Detroit	19,400
April 8	* Tony Musto	KO 9	St. Louis	17,468
May 23	* Buddy Baer	KO 7 † (Disq.)	Washington	36,866
June 18	* Billy Conn	KO 13	New York City	153,905
Sept. 29	* Lou Nova	KO 6	New York City	199,500
	Year: 7(7)-0 Career: 54(47)-1(1) Year: $466,892			
		1942		
Jan. 9	* Buddy Baer	KO 1	New York City	65,200
March 27	* Abe Simon	KO 6	New York City	45,822
	Year: 2(2)-0 Career: 56(49)-1(1) Year: $111,022			
		1943, 1944, 1945		
		In service. Exhibitions only.		
		1946		
June 19	* Billy Conn	KO 8	New York City	625,916
Sept. 18	* Tami Mauriello	KO 1	New York City	103,611
	Year: 2(2)-0 Career: 58(51)-1(1) Year: $729,527			

1947

Dec. 5	* Joe Walcott	W 15	New York City	75,968

Year: 1(0)-0 Career: 59(51)-1(1) Year: $75,968

1948

June 25	* Joe Walcott	KO 11	New York City	252,522

Year: 1(1)-1 Career: 60(52)-1(1) Year: $252,522

1949

Exhibitions only.

1950

Sept. 27	* Ezzard Charles	*L 15*	New York City	103,529
Nov. 29	Cesar Brion	W 10	Chicago	25,000

Year: 1-1 Career: 61(52)-2(1) Year: $128,529

1951

Jan. 3	Freddie Beshore	KO 4	Detroit	25,000
Feb. 7	Omelio Agramonte	W 10	Miami	16,309
Feb. 23	Andy Walker	KO 10	San Francisco	30,000
May 2	Omelio Agramonte	W 10	Detroit	25,000
June 15	Lee Savold	KO 6	New York City	28,266
Aug. 1	Cesar Brion	W 10	San Francisco	21,000
Aug. 15	Jimmy Bivins	W 10	Baltimore	24,557
Oct. 26	Rocky Marciano	*KO'd 8*	New York City	132,736

Year:73)-1(1) Career: 68(55)-3(2) Year: $302,868

TOTAL: $3,844,108

Plus approximately $1,500,000 exhibitions.

*—Title fight.
†—1941 victory by foul considered a KO.
‡—Louis donated $47,100 and $36,146 to Army and Navy Relief Funds.

JOE LOUIS'S TITLE FIGHTS

De-fenses	*Date*	*Foe*	*Site*	*Attendance*	*Gate*
	6-22-37	Braddock	Comiskey Park, Chicago	45,500	$ 715,470
1	8-30-37	Farr	Yankee Stadium	32,000	325,707
2	2-23-38	Mann	Madison Square Garden	19,490	111,71
3	4-1-38	Thomas	Chicago Stadium	10,743	48,19
4	6-22-38	Schmeling	Yankee Stadium	70,043	1,015,01
5	1-25-39	Lewis	Madison Square Garden	17,338	102,01
6	4-17-39	Roper	Wrigley Field, L.A.	21,675	87,67
7	6-28-39	Galento	Yankee Stadium	34,852	333,30
8	9-20-39	Pastor	Briggs Stadium, Detroit	33,868	347,87
9	2-9-40	Godoy	Madison Square Garden	15,657	88,49
10	3-29-40	Paychek	Madison Square Garden	10,609	62,48
11	6-20-40	Godoy	Yankee Stadium	26,640	164,12
12	12-16-40	McCoy	Boston Garden	13,325	51,01
13	1-31-41	Burman	Madison Square Garden	18,061	62,89
14	2-17-41	Dorazio	Convention Hall, Phila.	15,789	57,19
15	3-21-41	Simon	Olympia Arena, Detroit	16,003	54,76
16	4-8-41	Musto	St. Louis Arena	17,371	52,99
17	5-23-41	B. Baer	Griffith Stadium, D.C.	24,812	105,18
18	6-18-41	Conn	Polo Grounds	54,487	456,74
19	9-29-41	Nova	Polo Grounds	56,549	583,71
20	1-9-42	B. Baer	Madison Square Garden	16,689	189,70
21	3-27-42	Simon	Madison Square Garden	15,367	139,13
22	6-19-46	Conn	Yankee Stadium	45,266	1,925,56
23	9-18-46	Mauriello	Yankee Stadium	38,494	335,06
24	12-5-47	Walcott	Madison Square Garden	18,194	216,49
25	6-25-48	Walcott	Yankee Stadium	42,667	841,73
	9-27-50	Charles	Yankee Stadium	13,562	205,37

OTHER MAJOR FIGHTS

Date	Foe	Site	Attendance	Gate
6-25-35	Carnera	Yankee Stadium	62,500	328,65
9-24-35	M. Baer	Yankee Stadium	88,150	1,000,83
6-19-36	Schmeling	Yankee Stadium	42,088	547,54
10-26-51	Marciano	Madison Square Garden	17,241	152,84

INDEX